PEACE AND WAR

PEACE AND WAR

Growing up in Fascist Italy

WANDA NEWBY

COLLINS
London · 1991

William Collins Sons & Co. Ltd
London · Glasgow · Sydney · Auckland
Toronto · Johannesburg

First published in Great Britain 1991
Copyright © Wanda Newby 1991

BRITISH LIBRARY CATALOGUING IN PUBLICATION DATA
Newby, Wanda
    Peace and war: growing up in fascist Italy.
    1. Italy. Social life, 1918–1945 – Biographies
    I. Title
    945.0913092

    ISBN 0–00–215853–1

Phototypeset in Linotron Baskerville by
Input Typesetting Ltd, London
Printed and bound in Great Britain by
Hartnolls Limited, Bodmin, Cornwall

TO ERIC
who corrected my spelling

I would like to take this opportunity to
thank the following for all the help and
encouragement they gave me in writing this book:

My daughter Sonia Ashmore; my
godmother Danica Adamič; my lifelong
friends Lucia Pollanzi, Valeria Pizzi, Wilma
Botti, Ada Barantani, Pompeo Piazza, ex-mayor
of Fontanellato, and Maria Vittoria Ferrari;
and my editor Amanda McCardie for her patience.

CONTENTS

ILLUSTRATIONS

I

My Country and My People

La patria è un tutto
di cui noi siam le parti
Al cittadino è fallo
considerar se stesso
separato da lei.

HIDDEN IN the hills of the Kras, the limestone country above Trieste in Slovenia, which the Italians call the Carso, lies Kobjaglava, the village where I was born. No tourist ever went there and none goes there now. It is a small farming village, and more or less its only claim to fame is that it produces excellent *teran*, a dark, rather sharp red wine which is only made in a small area of the Kras. It is very good with Slovene food and said to be good for the health.

In this village almost everybody is related, and to this day there is no cinema or other place of amusement. Like all the other villages in the region it is dominated by the church with its tower, and on the outskirts is a small graveyard where some of my brothers and sisters are buried. I was the last of eleven and the only other survivor was my brother, the third-born.

My mother never told me how or why they died. I only know that they died either as soon as they were born or in the first months of their lives. Doctors were then few and far between up in the Kras, and covered very large areas. There were no telephones and antenatal care did not exist. During the Great War of 1914–18 the whole area was a gigantic battlefield. Perhaps it was partly because of the war that my mother continued to lose her babies.

My father was a schoolmaster, and just before the First

World War he was given a teaching post in Štanjel (in English St Daniel; in Italian San Daniele del Carso), a village ten kilometres or so away from Kobjaglava, where he had to live because accommodation was impossible to find in Štanjel and the schoolhouse was still occupied by the teacher he was replacing. Even in Kobjaglava it was difficult. The houses were small and the families large, as they usually included not only the parents and their children but also an unmarried brother or sister or both and the grandparents, who were the most respected members of the family. Nevertheless, a child-less couple took pity on my mother, who was in the last stages of one of her pregnancies, and offered her and my father a small house in their courtyard. It was certainly not a dream house but it made my mother happy, because it meant that she need not be separated from my father. It was in this house, many years later, that I was born. I arrived on a cold, windy, March day in 1922, so small an object that nobody thought I would live. The next November the schoolmaster's house in Štanjel became free and we moved there by horse-drawn cart, together with our few possessions.

We always remembered Kobjaglava; especially my mother, who left many friends there. During the next few years we paid them many visits and I, who had been too young to know them when we lived there, grew in turn very attached to them. It was a pretty village, whose narrow, unpaved streets were in contrast to the important-looking gateway with stone arches which led to the courtyard of almost every house, separating it from the outside world. When the big wooden doors were closed these gateways looked as if they shielded small fortresses.

The courtyards were spacious places with chickens roaming about in them. On one side there would be the cow shed with the hay loft above it, and on the other, at ground level, the wine cellar. Between them would stand the two-storey farmhouse, whitewashed every year. There was always a long balcony running the length of the upper floor, and when the long winter was over, it and the windows were miraculously filled with pots of geraniums, begonias, daisies and petunias, which gave the entire village an air of joy and happiness. Down in the courtyards would be large tubs of oleanders, always full of pink, red or white blooms. These always gave their owners mixed feelings of pleasure and regret if they had unmarried daughters, because in Slovenia people believe that where oleanders flower profusely the daughters will remain spinsters for ever. It was hard to believe, since we had been invited to numerous weddings in houses where the oleanders flowered in abundance.

The inhabitants of Kobjaglava, as everywhere else in the Kras, were extremely hospitable. Anyone who arrived from a neighbouring village was received with the utmost friendliness and I remember that when we came back to visit we had to consider very carefully which house to visit first in order not to hurt anyone's feelings.

When my mother and I set off on an outing to Kobjaglava, I never wanted the day to end. We set out early in the morning so that we could stop on the way in a field for a drink of cold coffee and some biscuits. In the shade of a tree my mother would tell me a story, then we would sing Slovene songs as we lay on the grass, watching the moving clouds and dreaming with our eyes open. In the hot weather the chirping of the cicadas accompanied our songs, just like a chorus.

The approach to Kobjaglava was unlike any other I knew. First we passed through a small oak wood where the trees threw great cool shadows on the road and formed a natural archway at the far end. Then the road continued through fields of *ajda*, a plant which in the late spring produces a sea of greyish-white flowers. These later turn into dark grey seeds

17

which can be ground up and cooked like porridge; the result is *ajdova*, a delicious sort of polenta to be eaten with meat stews. It was one of my favourite dishes.

Every family we called on received us in the kitchen, the friendliest room in the house, and immediately, unless it was lunch-time, we would be offered coffee and sweet bread with sultanas in it. The coffee was always made with hot milk, and I hated the skin floating on it. On the rare occasions when my father came with us he was always given a glass of home-distilled *žganje*, a fearfully strong drink like Italian grappa or French eau de vie, with his coffee. I was given a *malinoveč*, a delicious home-made juice of wild raspberries and sugar, to make up for the coffee.

'*Primi, lepa* – take it, beautiful. You must be thirsty after such a long walk,' they said. Other people's children were always called 'beautiful'.

These kitchens were immaculate. The stone floor was always kept scrubbed, and the big cooking stove shone like a mirror, polished every day. The stove, assembled by the local builder, had a door ornamented with brass, and a brass rail round the top. Usually there were four sets of rings, and a small copper tank for heating water at one end. If there were grandparents living in the house they had a comfortable seat near the warmest part of the stove but always facing the door, presumably so that they could see who came in. I have vivid memories of the old *teta* ('auntie'), wearing a scarf on her head, a very full, gathered skirt and equally full, gathered satin apron, all in black, leaning on the brass rail if the weather was chilly and extending her hands above the stove to keep them warm. To me these *tete* looked as old as the hills. Their faces were full of wrinkles and most of them had lost their teeth: when they laughed I could see only their bare gums.

Instead of a stove some families had an *ognjišče* – something

18

that has now almost completely disappeared. The *ognjišče* was the heart of the kitchen and of the family. A wood fire burnt on a platform near one of the walls, and suspended by a chain in the cavernous chimney above it was a copper cauldron so that there was always hot water; especially in winter, when the fire burned perpetually. There was a small window in the outer wall so that in the daytime you could keep an eye from outside on the fire and whatever was cooking.

On three sides of the *ognjišče* there were wooden benches with high backs. The *ognjišče* brought the family together in the evenings when there was time to talk, and very often the rosary was said; the oldest woman present would take the lead. The men of the family joined in, and removed their hats and caps (which most of them usually kept on, even indoors) as a mark of respect. The children were inevitably given the smokiest part to sit in. If they found it unbearable they went to bed.

Every kitchen in Kobjaglava had a wide stone shelf built into the wall on which stood ladles, glasses and an earthenware jug full of drinking water, so that anyone who was thirsty could help themselves. This water was drawn from the well in the courtyard, which went down a long way into the limestone of the Kras. In one corner was the *vintla*, a chest full of flour; it had a removable, reversible top which was used for kneading dough and bread-making. The best room, the equivalent of the front parlour (if there was one), was hardly ever used except on great occasions. It was a very simple room with a highly polished wooden floor. The large table would be covered with a pale-coloured cloth and surrounded by very upright chairs which gave the room a rather sad, forgotten look. There was also a dresser on which the best china was displayed, some of it perhaps quite old but hardly ever used, and wedding presents which were probably never used either. In one corner there would be a wooden

19

stand with an evergreen plant on it. The walls were stencilled in various colours and hung with family photographs in heavy, dark frames. The sitters, some of them taken on their wedding days in stark black and white, looked deeply solemn.

We were hardly ever shown the upstairs rooms. The only chance of seeing them was when a member of a family we knew was very ill or died, in which case we were allowed up to pay our last respects and bless the body, sprinkling it with holy water from a small branch of box which was kept on a table near the door. The body was always laid out on the bed on one of the family's best embroidered sheets, which originally formed part of the wife's trousseau and had sometimes been kept for three-quarters of a century for this purpose. The corpse would be dressed in deepest black, with black socks or stockings but no shoes. The hands were placed together as if in prayer, with the rosary held between the fingers. For as long as the body was exposed to view, neighbours and relatives would continue to say the rosary in turns, keeping company with the deceased and praying for his or her soul. I did not enjoy any of this but morbid curiosity always prevailed.

My mother would pass the rest of the day at Kobjaglava visiting and talking to her friends while I went with the children to the pastures. The older, more responsible children, when they were not at school, had the job of looking after the family's animals, which were never left unattended in the fields.

The fields were beautiful, and covered, according to the season, with all sorts of wild flowers – crocuses, snowdrops, narcissi, wild peonies, cyclamens and various kinds of orchid. We used to return to the village with our arms full of them. Nobody ever had any vases to put them in, so the cemetery was the only place for them; there were vases there, though never enough. On each gravestone in the cemetery was a photograph of the dead person, printed on a ceramic plaque. I always felt uneasy seeing the dead staring out at me from those stones, and I think the other children felt the same. Once we had set out the flowers we went straight back to the village.

Štanjel, where we went to live when I was a few months old, is made up of two villages: a very ancient upper village – virtually a little town – which remains more or less intact to this day, and a lower village, where our house was, on the main road from Trieste to Gorica. When I was small Lower Štanjel had a pond surrounded by a high wall, a *gostilna* (the local inn), a grocer's, a butcher's shop (which only opened twice a week) and a post office. Near the pond was a shrine erected in honour of the Holy Mary.

The upper village overlooks all the near and faraway hills and mountains of which Nanos, towards Postojna, is the highest. On the top, lost among the pine trees, a little white house was clearly visible. I remember wondering who lived in it. Could they be fairies or gnomes? I never wanted to ask because I preferred to keep my fantasies alive. The little house is still there, apparently unchanged, and I have still never been to it. I suppose it is a refuge for climbers or forest guards.

The most important building in Upper Štanjel is the castle, built by the Coblenz family in the sixteenth and seventeenth centuries, on the site of a medieval one. It was very badly damaged during the 1914–18 war, when it was a military hospital, held by the Austro-Hungarians against the Italians, and it was burned out in 1944 by the Germans and Fascists, who also burned many other houses in Štanjel and deported the inhabitants to Germany. This damage to the village was followed up by the Yugoslav partisans who burnt the castle once more in 1944, by which time it was nothing but a heap of rubble; it has since been rebuilt.

The church bore a charmed life. It was very badly damaged in the sixteenth century during the Turkish invasion – and later restored by a Count Coblenz, whose body was embalmed and buried in one of its tombs – but it survived both world wars without suffering serious damage. In spite of all its misfortunes Upper Štanjel is still one of the most beautiful villages in the Kras, as well as being the oldest.

I must have been about two years old when Štanjel was subjected to a number of severe earth tremors. They came late in the evening, quite suddenly. I was lifted out of my bed, wrapped in a shawl and taken out into the road where the other villagers were gathered, all very frightened. I saw our rooms moving and everything else shaking. For what seemed an eternity everyone waited outside, not having the courage to go back into their houses even after the tremors had long since died down. It was my brother who carried me into the kitchen and, seeing me pale and shivering, attempted to warm me by removing the shawl and sitting me on the copper lid of the hot-water tank of the stove, not realizing how hot it was. Nobody noticed until I began to scream and bellow with pain. For days afterwards I was unable to sit down, and the pattern of the lid remained impressed on my bottom for several weeks.

Štanjel was to be our home for the next nine years and I spent a very happy childhood there. We arrived on a freezing cold day when the *burja* was blowing full blast. The *burja* is a mercilessly penetrating wind which blows its hardest in the Kras and at Trieste and all along the shores of the Adriatic towards Venice, sometimes with such force at Trieste that ropes had to be put up in the city to prevent the inhabitants being whisked away by it. Up in the Kras, when I was small, horse-drawn wagons with heavy loads were sometimes blown

22

over and trains halted on the main line from Trieste to Ljubljana. Today the force of the *burja* is said to be much diminished, possibly because of reforestation further inland.

By comparison with our house in Kobjaglava, the one in Štanjel was positively spacious to my eyes. It was the upper part of the schoolhouse, which had been built at the beginning of the century on the site of a much more ancient building. When my father began digging a vegetable plot in the garden he found two Roman tear bottles and some fragments of Roman pottery.

The school was for boys and girls from the ages of six to eleven, and some of them came in from the surrounding villages, often some distance away. I clearly remember the boys and girls from Lukoveč, a small, very isolated hamlet high up in the hills to the north of Štanjel. Even when there was snow they used to walk to school, a journey of many kilometres. When the weather was bad they would set off earlier from Lukoveč so that they would have time to dry their clothes and get warm by the wood-burning stoves when they arrived. These stoves had long pipes which extended all around the room before discharging the smoke through chimneys in the side walls of the building. The longer the pipes were, the warmer the room would be. Under the house was an enormous, vaulted cellar with mysterious, cavern-like holes in the sides of it and small, high windows. This cellar had an ideal temperature for storing wine, cool in summer, warm in winter, because of the thickness of the walls, but my father never kept any in it because he didn't have a vineyard. Instead my mother kept chickens in it and they seemed very happy. In gratitude they laid large numbers of eggs.

On our own upper floor we had a kitchen, three large bedrooms, a landing that was no use for anything except playing and, at the very back of the house, a room my mother called the *kašča*, the attic, because it had a sloping roof. The

23

kitchen contained the usual wood-burning stove, a large table which my mother never seemed to be able to keep clear of objects (a defect which I have inherited), a dresser on which she displayed a quantity of glistening white plates, a very Middle-European white coffee set decorated with garlands of mauve flowers, of which she was very proud, and the two Roman tear bottles that my father had found.

The house was lit by oil lamps. The most dangerous ones were those that could be carried about; these were the most common cause of the fires which were frequent in this part of the world.

My brother and I each had a bedroom of our own but I didn't like sleeping by myself until I was much older because I was afraid of the dark, especially when the wind blew and moaned about the house like a lost soul. I was also a light sleeper, easily woken either by dreams or by the noise my mattress made when I turned over; it was filled, like everyone else's at that time, with maize leaves, which were supposed to be very good for the health of young children. Nights in our house were not exactly restful when I was little.

My favourite room was the *kašča*, which was the most fascinating place in the house. It was furnished with two large tables, a number of trunks full of old dresses belonging to my mother (which she allowed me and my friends to use for dressing up), quantities of old photographs, Austrian and German books which belonged to my father, and relics of the war – brass buttons, empty shell cases and my father's old army uniform. He had been an officer in the Austro-Hungarian army in the First World War and had been lucky enough to be given the job of carrying important dispatches across Europe, sometimes as far as Odessa. This kept him out of the front line and probably saved his life. He also managed to come home quite frequently – whether with official permission or not, I don't know.

The two tables in the *kašča* were always laden with various products, according to the season. In summer the bigger of the two was covered with silkworms for which endless quantities of mulberry leaves had to be gathered, and I could practically see them getting fatter under my own eyes. I was so much bigger than they were, but ate relatively much less: it was incomprehensible. Later the larva emerged and gradually got itself wrapped up with thin, intricate filaments of pale-yellow silk. I never really understood why my mother kept silkworms. I never actually saw her removing the cocoons and she never told me what she did with them. She must have sold them, but for me the point of these strange creatures, like their life cycle, remained a mystery.

The other table was filled with fruit and nuts put out to dry, or to be eaten in the winter months. At Christmas and Easter my mother used to spend several days making the sort of cakes that are traditional to the Slovenes, such as *pinca* – a sweet bread; *kugelhupf* – a very rich cake made with flour, butter, sugar, sultanas, eggs, milk and yeast; *potica* – rolled pastry filled with ground nuts, almonds, sultanas, sugar, pine kernels, spices, sour milk and rum; and *krapfen* – doughnuts – all of which took a long time to rise. Unless many visitors appeared on our doorstep these cakes could last for weeks, but unfortunately for me they tended to disappear very quickly – my parents were known for their generosity.

At Easter an extra table was put up in the *kašča* and was soon completely covered with *župca*, a thick jelly made from pigs' trotters and decorated with laurel leaves. *Župca* was one of the dishes I really liked (I still do), and sometimes I could not resist the temptation of dipping my finger in and spoiling the look of it. This made my mother absolutely furious, and for some days I would be in disgrace.

Hanging from hooks in the ceiling of the *kašča* were innumerable bunches of grapes, gifts from those parents of my father's pupils who had vineyards of their own. Although these had been cut in October when the harvest – the *bndima* (a corruption of the Italian *vendemmia*) – took place, they would all be kept until Christmas, by which time they would have shrunk and were much sweeter, more like sultanas.

The *kašča* had a large window which looked out on to the garden far below. Full of flowers and vegetables, this was a combined effort in cultivation by my father and mother – though they never gardened at the same time. When I was small I was never allowed in the garden during school hours in case I distracted my father's pupils, who would have liked to be out there with me in the open air rather than in the classroom. On one side of the garden was what we all called the *Gloriette*, a large wooden frame with a pointed roof, like a room without walls. Apart from the front, where the entrance was, it was completely covered with wild vines which pro- duced very sweet, small grapes to keep the birds happy. Why it was called the *Gloriette* I never bothered to ask. Now that I would really like to know I have been unable to find the word in French, English or German dictionaries. I think it must have been a legacy of my father's time in Vienna. Perhaps he visited Schönbrunn and saw, at the far end of the enormous garden, the colonnade known as the *Gloriette*, built on a hill by the architect von Hohenberg; though with its wonderful views of Vienna and the Wiener Wald it was a bit different from our own modest construction.

Near the house was a stone well in which we would some- times find tiny crabs and strange four-legged members of the salamander family – for the Kras is hollow. A few minutes after the most violent downpour the water would all have disappeared through cracks in the limestone into subter- ranean caverns. The ground's surface was full of holes, known as *kolisevke*, which looked like huge bomb craters, some as deep as three hundred feet, where the roofs of huge caves had

26

collapsed. A smaller sort, called *doline*, were funnel-shaped and anything up to sixty feet deep and three hundred feet across. These contained the best red earth. Here in the Kras, there were no natural earth fields. Men, women and children had worked for centuries literally weeding the ground of stones and piling them up in great mounds, then bringing earth in what must have been endless journeys by ox cart. All this to make a field perhaps thirty yards long, where vines, turnips, potatoes, maize, and the white-flowered *ajda* could grow.

My father was an excellent teacher. He was very determined and rather severe during lessons – at least he looked severe – and he expected good results from his pupils. He kept a small cane and very occasionally used it on one or two of the more undisciplined boys, none of whom ever wanted to repeat the experience. No parent ever complained as they probably would today, and when, many years later, I met some of his old pupils, they had nothing but praise for their Gospod Učitelji, their Mr Teacher, and remembered him with gratitude and affection. My father was a handsome man, and in spite of his severe aspect he was really very kind. He was an idealist (which was eventually to bring him into collision with Fascism), and although he enjoyed the company of his friends, deep inside he was a man who liked to pursue a solitary course – he was what now would be described as a loner.

In those days a teacher was considered rather an important person in a village like ours, and he had to be present whenever there was a function or a visit by an important official. On such occasions my father wore his best black suit; and he used to keep it on afterwards, much to my mother's displeasure. She was afraid he might damage it, sitting round an *ognjišče*, talking with his friends. Whenever possible he withdrew from these parties before they were over – unobserved, he hoped.

27

When, every two or three years, the Bishop of Gorica (Gorizia) came for Confirmation Day, a great arch made of branches of trees decorated with flowers and paper ribbons was erected in his honour across the road between Upper and Lower Štanjel. The building of the arch was a great event. Everybody was involved and gave a helping hand, and when the great day came the entire able-bodied population of Štanjel and the surrounding villages would be there.

My father loved the country and was at his happiest when he was out on the hills shooting, looking for mushrooms or wild asparagus, or searching for frogs at night with a torch. But an even greater pleasure for him was singing in choirs, or teaching choirs to sing in four voices. For the most part he taught Slovene songs, or extracts from operas.

The language we spoke at home was Slovene; not pure Slovene but a dialect known as Slovenska Špracha, widely spoken here where the Latin world ended and the Slavonic world began. We also spoke Italian; again not pure Italian but Triestino, the dialect of Trieste. Some of the people of Trieste used to come to Štanjel, either for a day's outing by train – Štanjel was on the line from Trieste to Gorica – or for holidays in summer, or for the shooting later in the year. All of them found Slovene very difficult and apart from a few useful words they never bothered to learn it.

Both my father and mother also spoke German well. My father, born in Volcjigrad in the Kras, learned his German in the high school in Gorica. My mother was born in Mavhinje, a Slovene village high above the sea between Trieste and Monfalcone, now very close to the Yugoslav–Italian border, but in Italy. Her maiden name was Urdih. My father married her when she was only seventeen, one of five children brought up by a widowed mother. She was a tall, erect woman who wore her hair in a bun and smiled very little. I rather suspect that this was because her teeth were not good, a very common defect at that time when dentists, like doctors, were almost non-existent in the Kras. It was said that the Empress Elizabeth of Austria, renowned for her beauty and her figure, was for the same reason never known to smile. My mother was very Victorian, deeply religious, with inflexible ideas and a will of iron; I find with dismay that I have inherited one or two of these characteristics. She demanded respect from her children, so much so that my brother always addressed her not with the confidential *ti* (you) but with the *vi* which is the equivalent of the German *Sie* or the French *vous*. In spite of all this disguise she had a very kind nature, and was generous and hospitable.

When she was young she was sent to live with the family of one of her uncles, who was a teacher at the high school in Zadar (otherwise Zara) on the coast of Dalmatia. There she learned to speak German, which was to prove very useful when later we were living in Italy under German occupation.

She had a good singing voice and in the evening, before I went to bed, she used to sing Slovene songs to me as lullabies:

> There, over the lake,
> down in the meadows,
> is the most beautiful place
> where my cradle was.
> She used to rock me,
> my sweet mother,
> and sing, 'haili haila'.

There was another about a little hill on which the sun always shone. 'I will take you there one day,' she used to say, as if the little hill really was a particular hill. In fact we were surrounded by hills as far as the eye could see and all of them looked happy and beautiful when the sun shone on them.

She did not have many books to read to me – mainly Grimm's fairy tales and some Slovene short stories – but there was one that I never wanted to read or hear read again. It was a thin, tall book which told the story of an ugly, thin, unsmiling man who was punished – I can't remember why – by being locked in a completely white room with nothing in it. He was not allowed to eat or drink or sing or look or think, and eventually he must have died. I can't remember. I could understand the not eating and drinking, and even the not singing, but I could not understand how he could not look or think. It worried me for a long time.

Of my brother I remember very little. He was eleven years older than I was and away at school in Udine in Italy; he lived with a family and returned home only during the holidays. His name was Ladislav, but everyone called him Slavko. He was a handsome, tall, blond boy with what would now be called a crew cut, and very Slavonic-looking. He was very affectionate towards me, but the gap in our ages was marked and I felt almost shy of him.

Music was my brother's great passion. When he was just eight or nine, he began to teach himself the violin, guitar and mandolin. Later he had lessons and was able to join the local band. In that way he earned a little money playing at village dances. My parents sometimes took me to the dances, especially those that took place in one of the few parts of the castle at Štanjel that were still inhabitable, and although I was little, my memory of them is very vivid. At the entrance, postcards were on sale which the young men bought and addressed to their sweethearts, or to the girls they liked the look of. During the evening the cards were sorted into piles and the girl who got the most was elected queen of the dance.

After the First World War a large part of what had been Slovenia under the Empire was annexed by Italy, and after Mussolini came to power in 1922 the rising tide of Fascism began to make itself felt. By the time my brother was an adolescent and had begun to have strong views about the

Fascist regime, life had begun to be very difficult for him and, as a result, for our parents too.

It was not only Slavko. Almost all the Slovene students who lived near what had been the border became suspect, and it was obvious that Mussolini would never come to any sort of reasonable arrangement with educated Slovenes, all of whom were endowed with strong nationalistic feelings. It must have been in 1928 that suddenly, in the middle of the night, Italian Blackshirts in civilian clothes woke my parents and searched the whole house, the school included, for subversive propaganda. Even the dirty-linen basket was emptied, and downstairs, in the classroom, all the papers and books were scattered about. This was the first of several such visits. The men left, as they came, saying not a word. My parents put a brave face on it while the search was in progress, but when it was all over my mother silently wiped away her tears. They both must have realized that there was going to be no future for my brother here; and that eventually he would be arrested. Slavko must have realized it too. By this time he was working as a clerk in the *opčina*, the town hall, at Štanjel. He decided to go to live in Argentina, where a large number of Slovenes had already emigrated, either to seek their fortunes or to escape Fascism, or both.

So, on a very cold, grey, misty day in November 1930, we all three went to Trieste to see him board the *Saturnia*, a big ship of the Cosulich line which was sailing for Buenos Aires. The ship was full of emigrants, who all stood on deck waving scarves, hats and handkerchiefs to their relatives and friends on the dockside, knowing that this would almost certainly be the last time they would ever see them; down on the dock there were a lot of tears shed. My parents behaved more as the British are supposed to in such circumstances than like Continentals; they kept on waving and smiling until the ship was far offshore and then were silent. I too, although I was only eight years old, was quiet. I too could feel the sadness and the tension, although I did not understand the implications of what had happened. Even I realized that a great change had just taken place in our lives.

Slavko wrote home regularly every month, always making life sound good even though he did have problems. He was fortunate in making a number of good friends within the Slovene community and eventually he married a Slovene girl. He earned his living by painting posters and by editing a newspaper which he started called *Slovenski Glas*, the *Voice of Slovenia*, which kept the national spirit alive among the emigrants and reminded them of their homes and relatives. Many years later, after the war, Tito invited him to Yugoslavia and offered him a post in recognition of his work; but he found the country so much changed that he no longer wished to stay in it. This was the last time I saw him.

My brother and his wife had two children: a boy, Nestor, and a girl, Hilda. Nestor was something of a prodigy: he learned to play the violin and gave his first public concert in Buenos Aires at the age of six. At the age of eighteen he was killed in a car accident. This misfortune left his parents – especially my brother, whose health was not good – desolate, and a year later Slavko died too.

Before we returned to Štanjel after seeing my brother off, my parents, probably not wanting the day to end on such a sad note, accepted an invitation from some friends to visit a sister ship of the *Saturnia* which was also lying in the docks.

We had never been in a ship before and I simply couldn't believe what I saw: cabins, some of them luxurious beyond belief, reception rooms, dining rooms, games rooms – a palatial new world. Our conducted tour ended in the kitchen where I was given what was to me a beautiful basket, made entirely of white sugar, with a long curved handle decorated with sugar daisies of various colours. Was it really for me?

Could I really take it home? My happiness was unbounded, and for the moment I forgot all the sadness of the day. For weeks I admired my basket and would not allow anyone else to touch it, but one day I dropped it and it broke. I began to eat the flowers, which lasted me for weeks, but the handle was as hard as rock. Eventually I got tired of all that sugar, and threw away the rest.

Alongside our house in Štanjel was a grassy lane. At the end of it was a gateway flanked by two stone pillars which gave access to the courtyard of a farmhouse. This was the home of Marija Karlutova, my best friend, and her young sister. There was a brother, too, who was away at a seminary studying to be a priest, and an old grandmother, a *stara mati*. Marija's father was dead and her mother had a terrible struggle, with only a little land, to make ends meet. Because of this there was not much time for Marija to come out and play. After school she had either to help in the fields or in the house – the cows had to be brought back from the pastures, wood had to be brought in, and there were innumerable small chores – so she was hardly ever free. She was only about eight, a little older than me. The family was so poor that as soon as the warm weather began Marija and her sister gave up wearing shoes and went barefoot. I rather liked the idea of this and tried it myself, but I was not used to the stones underfoot, some of which were razor-sharp and uncomfortably hot in summer, and I walked as though I was treading on eggs.

Weather permitting, the old grandmother used to sit on a chair near one of the stone entrance pillars, completely immobile, like a sentinel or a statue. She always looked extremely bad-tempered, and was invariably dressed in black from her headscarf to her black felt slippers. Every woman in the village at that time wore home-made black slippers – felt or cloth for weekdays, velvet for Sundays – and they wore high, laced boots in the fields.

The *stara mati* was rendered even more formidable-looking by the stout stick which she always carried. We were convinced that she kept it to use on us if we went close to her, because she gave the impression that she particularly disliked children, large or small. I kept as far away from her as possible.

Marija came to our house most often in the winter, when there was little to do in the fields, and we played in the *kašča*, which was spacious and private. 'You remember', she said one day, 'what your mother told you about babies and where they come from? Well, it isn't true. Mothers don't buy them from the *babca* [midwife]. Babies really grow in their mothers' bodies. What your mother told you isn't true.'

I was astonished. Was it possible? Should I believe Marija? Was my mother telling lies? I thought the matter over for several days and finally decided to pluck up my courage and ask my mother. 'I will take you to the *babca*, and prove to you that whoever told you such a thing was not telling you the truth,' she said.

The following afternoon I was taken to the house of the *babca*, which was near our own. She invited us into her large kitchen, and was obviously expecting us. She offered my mother coffee and me a raspberry juice. I knew her well and liked her. She always had a warm smile and was proud of showing her large number of gold-crowned teeth. As she was not old, she wore a light grey scarf and a grey cotton dress, which made her complexion, fresh as an advertisement for milk, even more pale. 'So you have come to see all the babies I have upstairs, all the babies I shall be taking to various mothers in the next few months,' she said. 'Just come upstairs and I will show them to you.'

Practically overcome with excitement I followed her up a

large, stone staircase that I had never seen before and on to a wide wooden landing where two tall, very *Mittel-Europ* wardrobes and three wooden chests stood. The great moment had finally come. Marija would have to believe me when I told her what I was about to see. But why were the babies not crying? The *babca* took a big bunch of keys out of her pocket and tried to open one of the chests. The key would not fit. She tried a second and a third, then all the remaining keys in turn, without success. She managed to achieve a worried expression. 'My husband must have taken the right keys and left me his by mistake, and he won't be back for three days. What shall I do? I've promised to deliver a baby tomorrow. I'm really sorry to have disappointed you but be sure that as soon as he comes back I will ask you to come here again!' She never did.

When I saw Marija I told her what had happened. 'Not only will you not see any of those babies because they don't exist,' she said, 'but when she mentioned her husband what she meant was her lover. I heard my mother and my grand-mother discussing that family when they thought I was asleep by the fire and not listening.' I didn't know what 'lover' meant, but I wasn't going to ask Marija.

Did my mother really tell lies? If she did, then I could tell them too. Slowly I started not to tell the truth myself, a habit which lasted almost until I was married.

Across the lane from the Karlutovi lived the Kovačevi family. The entrance to their courtyard was under a stone archway in the shadow of a tall mulberry tree. On one side of the courtyard was a large pile of logs, very neatly stacked, as if they had all been measured to exactly the same length, and at the far end was a barn filled with carts, ploughs, sickles, scythes, wooden rakes for hay-making, big, loosely woven baskets, hanks of rope, and harnesses. Overhead, high up under the roof, was the hay loft. The maize was kept either

in a big pile on the floor of the barn or in containers; but when it was first harvested it was left to dry in the sun for a few days before being shelled by the women or the old people. Ground up as flour it was used to make polenta.

Next door to the Kovačevi barn was the cellar, very dark and cool. Not surprisingly it was full of barrels: big, straw-covered demijohns; bottles – some of them very old and large, of a sort no longer made; small wooden hods for carrying grapes to the trough where they would be trodden underfoot; the trough itself; and a wine press. The doors had big locks on them which were opened by equally big hand-made keys that looked as if they might be several hundred years old.

Opposite the woodpile was the *hlev*, the cow shed, in which the Kovačevi kept their few animals. The milking was done by the grandmother, Teta Kovačeva, who could scarcely be seen at all when she was sitting almost underneath the cow on her little stool in the darkness. She was a small, thin person, dressed unusually in grey. Her grey headscarf framed a face with a kindly expression and a toothless mouth.

Separated from the cow shed by a small storeroom was the kitchen, with the usual complement of stoves and seats. It was the grandmother's responsibility to light the bread oven here and make the bread.

I not only knew which day it was that she made the bread – from the large bundle of wood to heat the oven which was left ready outside the kitchen door the evening before; I could also time the baking exactly from the moment the smoke began to pour out of the chimney as if from a steam engine. When I judged that the bread was nearly ready, I would appear on the doorstep and ask, '*z dovoljenjem*', permission to enter. Teta knew what I had come for. 'Here, you, I have baked you a *pogača*!' she used to say, and out of the oven she would take a flat, crusty, brown loaf, hot and steaming, that tasted more delicious than any bread I have tasted before or

since. Only Teta Kovačeva, so far as I was concerned, was able to bake bread of this unforgettable quality.

Strič (Uncle) Kovačev ran the farm, together with his son Pepi. The old man was tall with a large moustache; and he looked more like an Austrian army officer than a farmer. Unless the weather was hot, he wore a brown corduroy jacket which gave him an even more distinguished air, and I cannot remember ever seeing him without his Austrian-style brown felt hat. Pepi's wife was another Marija, and they had two children. Marija spent most of her working days in the fields whilst Teta Kovačeva did the cooking. Because Marija was a younger sort of *teta*, she wore her scarf tied at the back on the nape of her neck, not under her chin, and on her feet she wore thick, home-knitted mountain socks and high, lace-up boots like a man's. Teta Kovačeva only wore shoes on Sundays when she went to Mass, which she never missed, however tired she might be.

The great event of the year was the grape harvest, the *bndima*. The first grapes were picked in the nearest vineyard, the last in the one furthest away (where we live now in Italy we do it the other way round). The Kovačevi's most distant vineyard was over the deep, narrow valley of the Branica, a small river which flowed through it, one of the few above ground in the Kras. I was always asked to this *bndima* partly because the Kovačevi all knew I loved going with them and partly because, young as I was, I was a little older than their own children and might at a pinch help to keep them from drowning in what would be one of the rare deep pools in the Branica in October – if there was any water at all.

We would set off early in the morning while it was still cool, the children riding on a wooden cart pulled by two cows on a track that was downhill all the way and in some places really steep. There would be two carts, both full of wooden hods known as *biente*, but we were the only ones allowed to

37

ride. For us it was a terrifically exciting journey, especially at the steep parts where the animals almost began to gallop, giving us the feeling that they were out of control, which they more or less were.

'*Oila Mora!*' [who was the black cow] '*Oila! Oi, Oi, Oi! Oila Siva!*' [who was the grey one] Pepi shouted, trying to slow them down, while one of the other men who were coming to the *bndima* applied brake shoes to the cart, with little effect. Up in the cart we children, all of us in a sort of ecstasy of happiness, sang and laughed and uttered shrieks of pretend pain whenever the cart ran over a large stone.

Finally we crossed the Branica by a beautiful, high-arched stone bridge, at a point where it was about thirty feet wide – its maximum width – and entered the brilliantly green meadows which to this day have an Arcadian feeling about them. Over the meadows we climbed a little to the Kovačevi vineyard, which was on the far slope of the valley. When we arrived it was time for refreshments; just drinks, for we had already eaten a good breakfast of coffee, fresh bread and thick, dark honey produced by the Kovačevi bees.

What followed was a hard day's work for the Kovačevi and their helpers, for the harvest on the Branica had to be completed in one day. We children helped a little, or thought we did, and no one seemed to object if we alternated work with play. To us the Branica was an exciting river. In it and on its banks hours passed in what seemed an instant as we happily paddled, built dams, raced twigs downstream, made castles from the silvery sand and splashed one another.

When the time came to return to Štanjel everybody felt exhausted. It was hard for the animals, too. They now had to pull heavy loads of grapes up that steep hill, as well as carrying us.

By the time we got back it was already dark and the treading was put off until the following evening. During the day the barrels, which had been soaked in water for some while so that the staves could expand and prevent leakages, would be checked once more. The treading itself was generally done by four men. They rolled their trousers up to their knees and washed their feet, then got into the wooden trough and began to tread the grapes, first the red and then the white. They did it with rhythm, just as if they were dancing, telling anecdotes which made everyone laugh, stopping from time to time to drink a glass of wine (for this was thirsty work) and bursting into song:

> It makes me happy to drink the sweet wine
> and be in a good mood whilst I live
> and without worries
> . . . this makes me really happy.

The wine flowed freely, and as the evening went on everyone became more merry. When one lot of grapes was squashed enough they were allowed to run into the tubs, then emptied into the barrels where they would remain, juice, skins and stalks, until fermentation took place a few days later. The fermented juice would be poured into big barrels, and the remaining skins and stalks would be squashed with a press, each successive pressing producing wine of a lesser quality. These pressings went on until every drop of liquid had been extracted and what was left then, which resembled a sort of cake, was used to distil the spirit called *žganje*.

It was usually late at night before the treading was finished; by this time some of the men would be so merry that they could hardly stand up and their wives had to help them home. But no one ever became angry or violent; it was a happy evening for us all.

The road which ran past the Kovačevi was also the road to

Kobjaglava and at the beginning of it, just outside the village, a path led into a large green field with a few walnut trees growing close to the edge. In the middle of this field there was a muddy pond, relying on rainwater to keep it filled, where the animals used to drink on their way back from the pastures. There was also a small, single-storey house with permanently closed red shutters. It belonged to Angel, a bachelor who had lost one of his legs in the war. He had no artificial leg, only a stump which must have given him great pain at times; I often used to hear him groaning on the way home from the village, leaning heavily on a stick for support. His job in the village was to look after the public weighing machine, but he couldn't have been paid much to do this because the weighing machine was hardly ever used except in the autumn, when farmers weighed the firewood which they delivered to families who had none of their own.

We children were cruel to poor Angel. We made fun of him for no reason, knowing that he could not run, and he used to wave his stick in the air, shouting that he would not forget. Indeed he didn't. Our memories were far shorter than his, and if any boy or girl who had provoked him got too close he would seize him or her by the ear and use his stick, though not really hard. He would look the victim straight in the eye and shout, 'Do it again and I will unscrew your neck!' None of us ever complained to our families about this treatment because we all knew we were in the wrong and would be punished even more severely if the truth came to be known.

I often used to wonder what Angel lived on as he was never seen to do any shopping in the local shop; but whatever he ate he was certainly always thirsty. The *gostilna*, the local inn, was quite close to the weighing machine. In the summer he could usually be seen sitting outside it under a pergola, sip-

Myself aged eight

My father

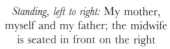

My mother with my brother Slavko

Standing, left to right: My mother, myself and my father; the midwife is seated in front on the right

Clockwise from the left: Myself, a friend, Lucia's mother and Lucia in Štanjel in around 1927

A family group in Kobjaglava

Lucia's father and mother
with me and Lucia (in front)

Lucia (left) and I with a now-forgotten
boyfriend

Lucia, myself and Max in the pastures

My brother with
a friend

My godmother Danica and I
at my confirmation

The well in Štanjel: Lucia is in the centre

Gospod and Gospa Gaspari

The motor car we filled with cow dung in Štanjel

ping innumerable glasses of wine, while in the winter he sat inside and saved fuel at home.

When he was over fifty, feeling perhaps unbearably lonely, Angel married, but unfortunately the marriage did not work. He returned to his bachelor life – the weighing machine and the *gostilna* – and from that time on the children left him in peace.

Opposite the midwife's house was the grocer's shop. Much more than a simple grocery; it was also an ironmonger's, a bakery, a haberdashery, and even a simple sort of chemist's shop – in fact it had everything a family needed. More important still it was a meeting place, not only for the village but for all the inhabitants of the smaller villages in the surrounding country as well. It was like a club, where the women, who often accompanied their husbands to Štanjel, could always find a customer for the eggs, fruit, chickens and vegetables they brought with them.

The shop was owned by Mr Kerševan and his wife Amalja. They were helped by their son Drago, a fat boy with a very red face who was much older than me and had already left school. He had to work hard because there was always a stream of customers, but his heart wasn't really in the job. He would have much preferred to play football outside with the other boys.

Drago had a nephew called Adrijan. He was about my age and he lived with the Kerševanovi because his parents, who lived and worked in Trieste, thought that the air of Štanjel would cure his pallor and lack of energy. In spite of his alleged lack of energy, Adrijan and I spent many happy hours together, playing hide-and-seek and climbing up the sacks in the storeroom. When Drago was alone and there was nothing much going on – the only time the shop was quiet was in the early afternoon – Adrijan and I pretended to be customers and wrote out orders for goods which Drago, who was really

41

very long-suffering and kind, used to prepare for us. Our orders were mostly for sweets or biscuits or dried fruit, and Drago wrapped them up for us beautifully in coloured paper. He insisted that what we had should be paid for with real money. Of course we had no real money, but outside the shop, beyond the storeroom, there was a large heap of earth where Drago used secretly to bury a few coins. He told us that long ago people had buried treasure there, part of which still remained. Filled with excitement we would scrabble in the heap and eventually always found some coins to pay our bills with.

The Kerševan shop was also an ideal place for children to catch diseases – measles, chickenpox and whooping cough – from one another, especially in winter when the stove was going full blast and the doors and windows were all closed.

Drago had an older sister called Danica and she was my favourite person in the whole of Štanjel. When I was five she was about twelve years old. She had few other friends because most of the time she was boarding at a convent school in Gorica, but during the holidays I became her chief amusement. She invited me to the house, she read to me, she told me long stories, she taught me to sew and draw and even began to teach me to play the piano, skills she had learned from the nuns in the convent. She also took me for walks and picnics, and one day she decided to arrange a surprise expedition for me and Adrijan. She didn't say where we would be going but we knew it must be somewhere with water because she gave us each a net; to catch butterflies and fish, she said. It could only be one place, I decided, and that was my favourite: the Branica.

We set off early, Danica carrying the picnic basket and towels while we carried the nets. The journey took rather a long time because our path down through the woods offered so many excuses to stop and look. There were wild strawberries,

42

beautifully coloured butterflies, wild flowers, and lizards we never seemed able to catch, however hard we tried. When we finally reached the river bank we stopped and stood in the green grass of the meadow, looking down into its crystal-clear waters, where lots of small fish were darting around, to the sandy bottom where dozens of little crabs, seeing our shadows overhead, were trying to hide themselves away.

'That's good,' said Danica. 'That's what we came for, to catch crabs, and we are certainly in luck today. I hope the basket I've brought to put them in won't be too small. Take off your shoes and socks and start netting.' When I ventured into the water I had the impression that there were hundreds of the creatures all around me. They had so many legs and moved so fast that I despaired of ever catching one, let alone enough to fill a basket; and if I did succeed in catching one, would it pinch me with its claws? I wanted desperately to be brave but I had the feeling that at any time one of them might run towards me and crawl all over me. The problem assumed enormous proportions and I stood there transfixed, seeing nothing else but crabs, crabs and more crabs, all getting bigger with every moment. I started to scream. Danica came to my aid, hoicked me out of the water and sat me down on the grass with my eyes shut. Meanwile Adrijan went on netting crabs, completely unworried by them.

'Perhaps it would be a good idea to have our picnic now,' said Danica diplomatically, and she started to unpack the basket; but it was no good. Although the food looked delicious I could not eat: those crabs had completely taken my appetite away. Soon we set off on the journey back to Štanjel. For the time being my enthusiasm for nature had evaporated and I walked back in silence; all I wanted was to go home.

That night enormous crabs tried to get me in my bed. They were everywhere – among the blankets and sheets and on the walls, always getting bigger and bigger – and my mother

43

could do nothing to calm me. Before long I was running a temperature, but eventually I fell into a deep, exhausted sleep. For the next two days I was kept quiet at home, and fishing for crabs was never mentioned again.

I had many nightmares, but the one I remember most clearly was connected with St Nicholas, the Slovene version of Father Christmas, who came at night to bring children presents on 6 December. The presents he brought were very small – sweets or coloured pencils wrapped in coloured paper. But on this particular 6 December I was told that he was going to be especially generous as some friends of my parents in Trieste had asked him to bring all the pots and pans for a dolls' kitchen and a bedroom set as well.

I could not wait for darkness to come that night, and when at last I was in bed I couldn't go to sleep for excitement. When would he come? Would he find me asleep? Would he open the window? St Nicholas never came down a chimney, but always through a window. It didn't matter if it was open or closed: he would always find a way in. My eyes were fixed on the window and suddenly he was there, suspended in the air – there was no sign of a ladder. He wore a bishop's mitre and carried a crozier in one hand and my parcel in the other, and he was staring at me. In spite of the parcel I was frozen with fear. I couldn't call out or scream, but I burst into uncontrollable tears. My parents heard me and came to me, but it took them a long time to calm me down. In order to do so they had reluctantly to tell me that St Nicholas, although he had existed once, was no longer alive, and that it was simply a tradition to make children believe in him. I was made to promise that I would never tell this secret to my friends and I kept my promise; but the vision of that apparition at my window always remained vivid in my memory.

Three years later, when the time came for my confirmation,

my parents asked Danica to be my godmother and she happily accepted. It was now that I came in contact with a real bishop, who looked just as St Nicholas had done that night. He seemed a kind man and smiled at us girls all dressed in white. We wore long white stockings kept up with elastic bands, white shoes, and white veils kept in place with little garlands of white waxed flowers, and each of us carried a candle in one hand and a prayer book in the other. I did not feel nearly as worried as I had on the occasion of my first Communion. Then our parish priest, who was rather old and severe, had told us that God would know if we omitted to confess any of our sins and punish us by causing a large hole to open in the ground and swallow us up.

As none of us had the courage to tell the priest about the 'rude' games we played, we were all convinced that Holy Communion day was going to be our last on earth, after which we would be frying in hell. During the entire Mass I shivered with fear, and two other girls were so overcome that they fainted. When the time came to take Communion I closed my eyes, waiting for the terrible moment, but nothing happened. To our surprise we were all alive.

Next to the Kerševanovi's house was the post office – just one large room in a house. The post office was the only place in Štanjel where financial transactions could take place, as there was no bank. The telegraph, with its constant ticking, used to keep the postmistress occupied for most of the day and the customers had to wait for ages before being served, but no one complained. Peasants are generally rather frightened of officials, even petty ones like a postmistress; and to make matters worse this one was old and severe. It was generally accepted that none of the letters that passed through her hands, either outgoing or incoming, ever did so without suffering some delay. Whether or not she ever opened any of them, as was popularly believed, no one now will ever know.

The large, very Slovene-looking house in which the post office and its forbidding postmistress were to be found was the property of Mr Gaspari, a thin man with a short white moustache. He inspired respect but it was impossible to imagine him smiling. He had held the post of mayor of Štanjel for many years, and only retired when he was too old to carry on. His wife, Teta Pepa, was younger than him and very able. She played a large part in running the farm and also took in paying guests from Trieste in the summer, most of whom came back faithfully year after year.

The Gaspari had two sons, Slavko and Max. Max was a tall, handsome, very dark boy who looked more as I imagined Albanians might, and was certainly nothing like a Slovene. He was three years older than me, and he hated school; his thoughts were on the world outside – the sky, the woods and their creatures – rather than on books and learning.

When I was five I was admitted to the lowest class of my father's school. I received no favours: quite the reverse. Altogether there were five different grades in the school; my father, who taught Slovene, and another teacher, who taught Italian, were responsible for all of them. It is difficult today to understand how they were able to cope with children of so many different ages.

Max was continually restless and succeeded in communicating his restlessness to others; as a result it was difficult for my father to keep the older boys in order (the girls were less trouble), especially if there was no real justification for punishment. One very hot day, when nobody could really concentrate, a bluebottle came buzzing in through an open window. Every eye followed it and it became impossible for the lesson to continue. My father always kept in his drawer a number of objects which he had impounded from the pupils.

46

Now he took out a catapult and challenged Max to kill the insect, offering a small round stone as ammunition. The suspense was almost unbearable. Max, in his element and happy to accept such a challenge, took the catapult and fired it at the bluebottle, which had momentarily settled on the wall. He missed.

Now it was my father's turn. His honour was at stake. He loaded the catapult with a second stone, waited for what seemed an eternity while the bluebottle continued to buzz around in mid-air, and then, the moment it alighted on the ceiling, shot it dead. There was a moment of intense silence. Then suddenly everyone was cheering; Max was defeated but he was cheering too. The lesson continued without any more interruptions, and my father never mentioned the incident again. He later became great friends with Max and used to take him hunting for frogs. Max would make fun of my father's white legs, telling him that they would frighten the frogs. I still remember the excitement of the time they brought home eighty, just the two of them.

Max knew so much about life in the woods. He knew where the nests were, and where to find deer, hares and squirrels, but he would never harm any of them as some other boys did. He often took sick animals home and nursed them until they were fit to fend for themselves again. He once kept an entire family of birds that had been abandoned by their parents and let them go in the woods when they were old enough to fly safely. He always carried a knife, except when he was at school, where knives were forbidden. It was very sharp and shaped like a miniature sickle, and he never allowed anyone else to borrow it.

In the winter he felt like a prisoner. The days were short, and because of the wind and the cold, which was sometimes intense, he could not stay outside for long. He sat around the family *ognjišče* to keep warm and used his knife to carve all sorts of objects – whistles, and the best catapults I ever saw.

It was during one of these evenings around the *ognjišče* that Max stood up to imitate the flight of a bird. Holding his knife open in one hand, he was just swinging round when I appeared in the kitchen. It all happened so fast that he couldn't avoid my cheek, and the knife blade went in, producing a half-moon cut from which blood started pouring in large quantities. The scar remained visible for many years.

In the summer Max and I and some of the other children used to go to the pastures after school. He took turns with his brother to drive the animals out and watch over them while they grazed. They were many fields belonging to different families, and they were divided from one another by drystone walls which were always being broken down. If one of the animals found an opening it was easy for it to escape and start eating in another field, a practice which was not particularly popular with the owners, however friendly they might otherwise be.

There was much to amuse us during these late afternoon hours. On breezy days we flew home-made kites that we had learned how to make at school. We had contests for the best kite or the one with the most beautiful colours. The wind lifted them up and up, as high and as far as the string allowed, taking with them our thoughts, our hopes, our hearts, our eyes, our outbursts of joy at seeing them flying so beautifully – everything that we had to offer went with them into the sky. If the wind was too strong for our flimsy string it would break, while the kite flew higher and higher and sometimes disappeared for ever into the clouds. Then it was as if a part of ourselves had gone.

In those fields and in other parts of the Kras there were still trenches left over from the 1914–18 war. It had been one of the worst battlefields from the point of view of the injuries sustained, because it was all rock, which fragmented into thousands of deadly pieces when a shell hit it. Most of us knew quite a lot about what that war was like up here on the Kras, having listened to fathers and uncles who had fought in it, so our games had more than a touch of reality.

The boys were the soldiers; some were Austro-Hungarians, while others had reluctantly to be Italians, the enemy. They faced one another in trenches that were only about ten metres apart. On their heads they wore old, rusty helmets which we found scattered around everywhere, and they brandished either wooden bayonets which they had made themselves, or the rusty remains of real ones. They 'bombed' one another with stones while the girls pretended to cook for them, using empty sardine tins as pots, and broken knives, forks, spoons, plates and aluminium water bottles which we had found half-buried in the ground. Some of us became nurses and attended the wounded, using old bits of rag as bandages.

Most of those who died in the 1914–18 war were buried in a special military cemetery down in the valley below Štanjel, not far from the railway station. Perhaps that particular spot was chosen so that anyone travelling by train would see the simple stone crosses over the graves and remember them:

> Go, tell the Spartans thou who passeth by
> That here obedient to their law we lie.

When the winter was nearly over but there were still traces of snow on the ground, the first snowdrops would appear in the cemetery, as if to pay tribute to all the young men buried there. There were Italians, Austrians, Slavs and Jews, and I particularly remember one named Desko Stainer because he was so young – just sixteen years old. I once saw a farmer working in a nearby field turn towards the cemetery, make the sign of the cross and say a prayer, but hardly anybody came to see it except on Armistice Day. Then the local authorities came to pay tribute, and our priest came to bless the graves and say Mass.

Perhaps the parents of these dead soldiers did not know where their sons lay buried, or perhaps they lived too far away ever to visit them. I hoped my short visits, even if they were only to pick snowdrops, provided a little company. The only other flowers that grew there were lilies of the valley. I never picked these because they grew among the brambles, which seemed to be there to protect them.

The cemetery still exists, but apart from the principal memorial which lies close under the hill, all the crosses were removed under Mussolini. A few have been broken up and piled in a heap in the nearby bushes. There is no fence, and cows feed among what were once the tombs. The bodies were taken to the war cemetery Mussolini had built up at Redipuglia, near Monfalcone, which is in the form of an enormous staircase ascending the slopes of the Kras.

Besides food and drink the *gostilna* was licensed to sell tobacco, salt and quinine – all Italian state monopolies. My father was a fairly regular customer: he would buy his cigarettes there, then stop on for a glass or two of wine and a game of *briškula* ('Trumps'), a very popular card game which resembled whist.

One Good Friday evening when I was about five years old, my mother left me in bed in the charge of my father while she attended the Stations of the Cross in the church. I had fallen asleep and my father, realizing he had run out of cigarettes, decided to go quickly to the *gostilna* and get some – it was only a few yards away. While he was out I woke up and, not hearing any reply to my shouts, went to the window and looked out to see a strange light, followed by flames, coming from the inn. People ran out of their houses shouting, 'It's burning, it's burning!'

50

The next thing I remember is the inn-keeper's daughter jumping out of a first-floor window into a large blanket that my father and others were holding outstretched for this purpose. Then he came running back to the house, wrapped me in a blanket and took me out into the street where the strong wind was fanning the flames. Very little could be done to quench them as there was no fire brigade, only one or two old, very leaky hoses. Meanwhile the alarm had been given in the church where the rest of the inn-keeper's family, the Šnajderjevi, were, and the entire congregation poured out into the street, horrified by what they saw. It was said that a spark from the chimney had set the house on fire. This was quite a common happening in the Kras, where so many of the houses were made of wood. For the Šnajderjevi it was really a terrible misfortune. They had lost almost everything they possessed. To our small community the *gostilna* was such a serious loss that about six months later it was entirely rebuilt.

For the rest of that evening, while my parents tried to help in whatever way they could, I stayed with Rosalia Bogateč and her family. I liked them all, especially their daughter Ida who was about my age, a very thin, tall girl with a complexion so pale that her dark fringe made her look quite ill. In front of the house there were long wooden benches to sit on with tubs of the most wonderful oleanders at either end; they always seemed to be in full flower.

The family had the biggest herd of cows in Lower Štanjel and this was the source of their income. Rosalia and her husband used to get up very early each morning to do the milking, and the milk was then put into little aluminium churns that fitted in a large basket which she carried on her head. She balanced it on a small cushion with a hole in the middle to make it more stable and comfortable. With one hand free for an emergency and another churn in the other, she walked every morning to the railway station where she caught the first train to Trieste, so as to be in time to serve her customers. She was a handsome, robust woman with a continuous smile which showed a number of golden teeth. Because of the great weight she carried on her head she always walked very erect, her hips moving with a rhythm which made her full skirt swing rather like a kilt.

She also took her customers her potent home-made *žganje*. The quantity permitted was controlled by the customs at the station in Trieste, whose officials often stopped her and others like her, but she used to get over this problem by hiding a couple of bottles under her ample skirts and petticoat.

The road leading to Upper Štanjel was unpaved and climbed gently along the side of the hill beneath the walls of the castle. It was used by horse-drawn carts, animals coming in from the pastures and the children who accompanied them, invariably carrying bundles of kindling wood on their heads. The road was shaded by plane trees on the outer side, while on the inner, a high stone wall concealed terraces which must have been part of the original gardens of the castle; now there was a vineyard there. About half-way up on the left was a secretive-looking gate that was always kept locked. It led into a demesne which more or less surrounded the whole of Upper Štanjel and the castle hill, and was the property of the Fabiani family. This was the only wealthy family in the whole of Štanjel, and they lived in a large, recently restored house on the other side of the hill with magnificent views over the Branica valley. I often stopped in front of the gate, hoping to find it open and wondering what mysteries it concealed. Certainly there were beautiful ladies in long flowing dresses, who walked along the paths while their children played and picked flowers under the watchful eyes of nannies. Such people really did exist, I knew, because on rare occasions during their long summer stays with the Fabianis, I had seen them. The older children were very well behaved and tidy, and usually spoke German, while two smaller children were pushed by a nanny in the only perambulator the village had ever seen.

The road entered the upper village through a tall stone archway, part of the fortifications built at the same time as the castle, in the second half of the sixteenth century. Immediately on the left of the archway there was a flight of wide stone steps which led up into a little square, the heart of Upper Štanjel, where the castle and the church (which had a spire like a medieval rocket) were to be found.

The Secretary of the Municipality was Bogomil Čehovin, a distinguished-looking, well-educated man who was also a good friend of our family. He lived with his wife, Franciška, in a large house down in the valley of the Branica. He also owned the hills around the house, which were always intensely green because they were so near the river. They were cultivated partly as woods and partly as vineyards: Čehovin wine was well-known for its excellent quality, due to the sheltered, sunny position of the vines.

The house itself was very simple, although quite large, and was used partly as a *gostilna*; the pergola in the courtyard gave shade to customers and friends of the family alike. Passers-by and villagers used to stop for a glass of wine and a snack of delicious home-baked bread and cheese or the home-cured, smoked ham of the Kras, called *pršut*. Mrs Čehovin was a tall, dark, handsome woman who not only ran the inn in the daytime, but also dealt with the everyday problems of the farm.

In front of the Čehovin house, in a very prominent position so that it could be seen for miles, was a tall white statue of Mr Čehovin's great-uncle, General Baron Andrea Čehovin, who was born in Branica in 1810 and died at Baden near Vienna in 1855 after a most distinguished military career. He played an important part in the battles of Livorno, Sommacampagna, Mortara and Montanara in Italy against the Italians, and behaved with great gallantry. It was the Emperor Franz Joseph of Austria himself who decorated the Baron with the Highly Distinguished Cross and had the statue erected as a monument, with its inscription: 'To the Bravest of the Brave'. During the Second World War it was damaged by Fascists, who smeared it with tar, and to avoid further vandalism the Čehovini had it buried in their kitchen garden, leaving (presumably by mistake) the toe of one boot sticking out of the ground. It has recently been restored, and the Baron now stands once more in his original position, high on a pedestal. He wears a uniform covered by a large cloak, but the hand which originally held his sword is empty now.

Mr Čehovin used to have his midday meal with us every day and sometimes, if the weather was very bad, he used to stay the night in his office in the Municipality, not wanting to venture out into the cold, wet darkness on his old motorcycle. Once, because the snow had fallen heavily, he stayed with us for three nights without being able to communicate with his wife. By the fourth day Franciška got so worried that she saddled a mule and, braving the icy weather, set off for Štanjel to find out what had happened, only to discover her husband working away as usual in his comfortable, warm office.

The houses in Upper Štanjel were all built on terraces cut into the side of the hill, some of them reaching as high as the rooftops, which meant that there were no gardens of any kind behind them. The lanes that ran in front, where chickens roamed and cats stalked, were unpaved and extremely narrow, and one level was often connected with another by a flight of steps. Three of these led up into small squares which were popular meeting places.

I had only one friend in Upper Štanjel, a girl called Slavica who had the misfortune to be permanently lame in one leg.

She lived in two rooms with her mother, who looked so old that she resembled a witch. Perhaps she was a witch, but she had a heart of gold, although she was terribly poor. She was always cheerful and insisted on sharing whatever she had with any visitor who came. Their house was so dark that it seemed like perpetual night there, and I think it was also the poorest house I ever knew. In the kitchen was a table and four rickety chairs, a small stove for cooking and a small stone sink from which the water was drained away into a bucket, and that was all. In place of a lavatory they used the cow shed under the house where their two cows were housed. I never saw their bedroom.

I don't know how they managed to feed and clothe themselves but I suspect that their neighbours were kind to them. I didn't often go to see Slavica, not because she was poor but because to me Upper and Lower Štanjel, although no more than 500 metres apart, were different worlds.

My sense of this was increased when I ventured to join in Upper Štanjel games, although, as a friend of Slavica's, I was accepted without question. These games were always exciting, very different to those we played in the fields. We chased one another through dark, ghostly alleys and explored old, uninhabited houses, and I invariably lost myself in real labyrinths. None of the girls here had such a thing as a doll. No one had toys unless they made them themselves; their greatest luxuries were rubber balls. It made me feel very lucky because I actually possessed two dolls, which were kept sitting in my bedroom and hardly ever played with. One, which I still have, was a celluloid doll brought from Japan by a sea captain. But when I was in Upper Štanjel I kept quiet about my dolls.

For me Štanjel was a paradise, especially during the summer holidays when families used to come up from Trieste with their children. They came year after year and stayed in the same houses, hiring the same rooms. The letting of rooms was an important part of the village economy.

Among these visitors were Lucia and her mother. Lucia's father appeared only very rarely because he was a sea captain in the Italian merchant marine, away for months at a time. When he did come to Štanjel he used to wear a dark-blue blazer with brass buttons, white trousers, white shoes, a peaked cap with a white piqué cover and a monocle, all of which created a profound impression.

Lucia and her mother took rooms in the mayor's house and took their meals in the inn. Lucia's only interest was in animals, especially dogs and cats. At home in Trieste she looked after twenty-five cats, none of which actually belonged to her, while in the apartment itself she was allowed to keep twelve canaries which she looked after beautifully, feeding and cleaning them all every morning before she went to school. Each one had a name and, as I discovered when I went to stay with her, they all seemed to know her voice. When Lucia and her mother came on holiday a trusted and heroic neighbour took over the job of looking after them – all but two cages of birds from which Lucia could not bear to be parted and which she brought on holiday with her.

Lucia, her mother, the canaries and the cabin trunk all came to Štanjel by train, and as there were no taxis at the station three local boys would be deputed to help carry the luggage. I would learn from them of Lucia's imminent arrival and set off immediately for the station to wait excitedly for the puffing steam engine which would bring both Lucia and her present. The present was always the same: a box of real Turkish delight which her father used to bring back from his travels.

Lucia was Italian and she spoke the Triestino dialect; correct Italian was only taught and spoken in school. Although she came to Štanjel year after year she never made any effort to learn Slovene. When I asked her why, she answered that in Trieste there was no use for our language and that it was too difficult for her to learn anyway. But the real reason was a different one, I think. In Trieste, where the population was a mixture of Italians, Germans, Austrians, Jews and Slovenes, the Slovene people were regarded as an inferior race. Many times, both when I was young and when I was older, I heard the word 'slaves' – *sciavi* in Triestino, *schiavi* in Italian – used by Triestini to describe us.

Whatever the reason may have been, she never made friends with any of the children in Štanjel apart from me and Max, with whom she shared a common love of animals. There were a number of dogs in the village, many of them ferocious because they were always kept on a chain; Lucia knew them all, and visited them regularly.

Accompanied by her mother, Lucia and I spent many days in the woods together, often in my favourite pine woods overlooking the Branica. There was always a delicious breeze there, even on the hottest days, and the smell of pine resin was particularly pungent. We would set off in the morning. Lucia's mother would bring a parasol, a basket containing a delicious picnic, and her knitting, and we would carry out butterfly nets, our spades, and a hammock in which the Signora could rest when she got tired of knitting. (Slinging the hammock between two trees was the most complicated operation imaginable.) Lucia and I would build small huts with pine branches and dig tunnels which we tried to train beetles and ants to use; unfortunately they never wanted to. We chased lizards, grasshoppers and butterflies; once they were netted we kept them in captivity for a short time before releasing them. The only insects we left severely alone were spiders, of which we were both terrified. All in all the wildlife of the pine woods of Branica must have been very relieved when we finally packed up and went home.

Among all the visitors to Štanjel was a family who used to stay in our house. They usually came in the late autumn and winter for the pheasant-shooting, when all the others had departed, but they would sometimes come just for a day's outing in the summer. They always arrived in a large open motor car, of the sort that I now recognize, having lived in England for many years: it was one that Mr Toad would have stolen if he had had half a chance. They always arrived wearing very smart leather motoring coats and hats fastened under their chins to stop the wind blowing them away; and, most important of all, they brought me presents.

During one of their visits Lucia persuaded me that we should put some cow dung in their car while no one was looking; there was a huge pile of it in the Kovačevi's field nearest the house. We scattered it all over the beautiful leather seats and the deep-pile carpet, but when we thought that we had done enough a terrible feeling of guilt, the sort of guilt I had felt when the priest had told me about the gaping hole in the ground which would swallow me up, came over both of us.

What could we do? To us there seemed no alternative but to hide, and as near the bowels of the earth as we could possibly manage. The caves in the woods were too far off, and the trenches on the hillside too open, so two trembling figures took refuge in our cellar, and shared it uneasily with my mother's chickens. We sat there on the damp earth all through an endless afternoon, and felt very hungry.

Meanwhile our parents had been searching for us high and low (but not low enough) and, knowing by now that they were looking for us, we decided to give ourselves up. When we appeared they were so relieved that punishment was reserved until later. Of course we were made to apologize to the owners of the car, which we did, but they seemed to find the whole affair rather funny. At any rate, they never stopped bringing me presents.

When I was about eight years old a new schoolteacher was appointed in Štanjel to assist my father. He and his wife could speak Slovene, but the three children, two girls and a boy, could not speak a word; up to this time they had lived in an Italian-speaking community. They quickly learned. I soon became good friends with Ester, the eldest, but her brother Silvano was more difficult to get to know. He was a year older than me and hardly ever joined in our games. He was very handsome, with dark hypnotic eyes, and withdrawn, always far away with his thoughts. He was very intelligent, always top of his class, and on the rare occasions when he laughed it seemed as if the whole world was laughing with him. When he did speak, he told us of extraordinary adventures that had befallen him in a world that certainly did not exist, although we believed in it; he must have read about it in books.

One day he suddenly became very argumentative, and nothing the rest of us could say or do was right. In revenge, trying to hurt him in the cruel way children sometimes have, I started to call him by the hated nickname he had had when he was small – Pupo, which means 'doll' in Triestino. He gave me a look of absolute hatred, grabbed a thick stick which happened to be handy, and hit me on the head with it with all his strength. That was the last thing I knew until I came round, in bed. In spite of this incident we became the best of friends and when, two years later, he and his family left Štanjel, it was Silvano I missed most.

Many years later, when we were living in Italy, I saw a lonely but somehow familiar figure sitting on a bench in a tree-lined street: it was Silvano. We recognized each other immediately, and in my eyes he hadn't changed at all; he still had his hypnotic eyes and his sad, enigmatic smile. He stayed with us for a few days and then disappeared without a word. I didn't hear from him again until he telephoned me in Wimbledon thirty years later. He came to see me, but told me as little as ever about the real Silvano, and refused to be questioned. He just told me that the death of his father, who had gone to work in Africa after leaving Štanjel, had left him very lonely and that he was convinced that his mother, who was also a schoolteacher, had no affection for him. He was now a qualified doctor and lived in the woods around Rome, in a tent, trying to help people who needed him and couldn't help themselves. His visit was very short and he disappeared from comfortable Wimbledon as swiftly as he had come. I have not heard a word from him since.

II

First Steps in Italy

SOMETIME in the early thirties Mussolini issued orders that large numbers of civil servants – including school-teachers – of Yugoslav origin, employed in the parts of the country ceded to Italy after 1918, should be removed from their posts and literally deported to live among Italians in Italy, because the regime did not trust their loyalty. Already our friend Mr Čehovin, the Secretary of the Municipality, had been transferred to Padua, leaving his wife and family to carry on running the *gostilna*. A number of teachers had been sent away from our area, too; some of them as far away as Naples. Students held secret meetings and there were rumours of plots to assassinate Mussolini, but these always failed, and it was said that those involved were given long prison sentences or suffered a worse fate.

All we ever heard in Štanjel was hearsay. There were no secret gatherings, partly because there were hardly any students, and because the peasants and artisans, although very anti-Fascist, had no desire to be caught up in political activities. In the spring of 1932, when I was ten years old, we heard rumours that my father was to be transferred to Italy. In those days country people were not used to travelling, and anything beyond Trieste or Gorica was almost unknown to the inhabitants of Štanjel. Southern Italy, to which some of my father's colleagues had been sent, was infinitely remote, another world. Rumour became reality when my father received a cold, official letter telling him that he was being sent to a place called Fontanellato. We studied the map to discover that this was a village near Parma, a city in what is known as the Pianura Padana, the great plain in northern Italy through which the River Po flows on its way to the Adriatic.

This came as a great shock to my parents, especially my mother. Neither of them was young, and the thought of going to a place where everything including the language was different – apart from Slovene and German they spoke only Triestino – cast a deep gloom over them; but they had no choice. Worst of all, it was going to be extremely difficult for my father to teach Italian to Italians, which would be his job.

The order came at the end of the summer term and, just as the holidays were beginning, the teacher who was going to replace my father arrived to see what kind of strange specimens he was going to land among and what sort of house he and his family were going to live in. A southern Italian, he had taught up until now in a village near Naples and could not speak a word either of Slovene or of Triestino. He must have had the same kind of feelings as my father had at the prospect of being sent to Fontanellato. In the event, inhabitants of Štanjel, although they were certainly not unkind to him, did not exactly welcome him with open arms. They regarded him as something more or less from outer space, and it was a long time before he and his family felt themselves to be part of the community. As no temporary accommodation could be found for him in Štanjel my parents gave him a room in our house; his family joined him there when we left.

In September my father set off for Fontanellato to find somewhere for us to live, just as the teacher from the South had done. Although he had anticipated all sorts of difficulties, he found a flat to rent. It was on the outskirts of the village and belonged to an elderly, childless couple. He sent a telegram to my mother telling her to get ready and pack.

A few days later he came to fetch us. He seemed quite cheerful. Everyone he had met in Fontanellato had been very kind, a good deal kinder than the people of Štanjel had been to his successor; which was encouraging. A lorry was hired to carry our furniture and other belongings to Fontanellato, not an easy thing to arrange at that time as there were few local drivers willing to travel so far. We ourselves were to travel by train. For a week we went from door to door, saying goodbye to all the families we considered as our own because we had lived among them so long. I saw my mother crying on several occasions.

On the day of our departure all our close friends came to the railway station to see us off. They brought presents of ham, nuts, cakes and bottles of wine for the journey, most of which we couldn't possibly take with us as we had no room in our suitcases. I felt rather like an explorer being seen off into the unknown. As the train drew out our dear friends on the platform blew kisses, shed tears and waved their handkerchiefs. Although I was sad to leave them, I was also excited at the thought of the long train journey ahead, and the thought of Italy.

In Trieste we changed trains and took the express to Venice. After it had run along the shores of the Adriatic on its way to Monfalcone, I had my last view of the Kras, the country in which I had been born, rising like a great wall above the plains of Friuli and then gradually disappearing altogether. Many years were to elapse before I saw it again.

We arrived in Venice with time to spare before catching

the train to Bologna, where we would have to change a third
time for Parma. My mother volunteered to look after the
luggage while my father and I went for a short walk. It was
early morning and I was overwhelmed by the magic of
Venice. It appeared so beautiful and silent, as if it were
asleep, with the windows on its balconies still closed. Only a
few gondolas glided past, and in the distance barges laden
with fruit and vegetables were being taken to a market. From
time to time a bell sounded from a campanile, adding to
the enchantment of the hour. The houses looked completely
different from those in Trieste, most of which were grey and
severe, and although I had seen picture postcards of Venice
nothing could have prepared me for what I now saw for the
first time from the steps of the railway station.

We arrived in Parma in the late afternoon, and found the
car my father had ordered waiting to take us to Fontanellato.
It was late September, and children playing in the streets
gave the city an air of holiday as we travelled through the
outskirts of Parma.

Soon we were on the Via Emilia, the great, straight Roman
road that runs diagonally through the *pianura* from Milan to
Rimini. After driving a few miles along what seemed an
endless avenue of poplars we crossed the Taro, at this time
of year a dry riverbed, by a long bridge with marble statues
of reclining river gods and goddesses at either end. Then we
turned off into the heart of the plain at Ponte Taro, a small
hamlet, for the final stage of our journey.

Everything seemed very different from what I was used to.
The houses, scattered in the countryside, looked enormous,
like fortresses, with large barns and farmyards attached to
them, and all the buildings were an ochre colour which made
them very beautiful in the evening sunshine. The fields were
vast, full now of dark-yellow wheat stubble, waiting to be
ploughed. They were interspersed with rows of vines, whose

66

high branches must have made the harvest very hard work. In the Kras the vines grew close to the ground, and the fields were tiny and defined by stone walls, while in the Po valley there seemed to be no walls at all.

That evening I did not see anything of Fontanellato because our new home was on the outskirts of the village and we drove straight there. It was an elegant small house on two floors, painted in pale green with dark green shutters, and we were to live in half of it, up and down. We came into the garden through a small wrought-iron gate under an arch of beautiful white roses, some of which were still in flower. The owners, the Signori Grignaffini, gave us a warm welcome before showing us our new home, and then insisted that we should have supper with them. The signora was a white-haired lady in her sixties, very thin and slightly bent, with a wrinkled face and a large number of gold teeth, while the signore was almost completely hidden from view behind the biggest stomach I had ever seen. None of the men in Štanjel had anything like it. Most of them were on the lean side because of the hard life they led and the long walks they took over hilly country to reach their fields.

Signor Grignaffini was a wealthy man. He earned his living as a *mediatore*, a middle-man in the farmers' buying and selling of livestock. He used to cycle from village to village visiting farms to inspect the animals, then on market days he would try to conclude deals between the farmers. When the weather was cold he would wrap himself up in a *tabar*, a big, black, woollen cloak. In the spring, when the air was still cool, he wore one of a lighter weight and colour. These *tabarri*, worn by most men in the region, kept the body and the hands very warm. They were worn with one end thrown across the shoulder high under the chin, giving the wearer a conspiratorial air. In spite of all the exercise Signor Grignaffini took on his bicycle he never lost any weight: food and wine were too great a temptation for him.

The next day I ventured out to see our new village, conscious that many curious eyes were on me. I remember hearing one or two voices saying, '*E'la figlia del nuovo maestro; sono Tedeschi*' – 'She is the daughter of the new teacher; they are Germans.' I could not understand at the time why they thought we were Germans, but I later discovered that they knew we were people from a border and the only border they could think of was the one with Austria, which for them was the same as Germany. Yugoslavia was unknown to them.

Fontanellato was a village of arcaded streets. All the shops and cafés were sheltered under the arcades, and I found I could walk almost the entire length and breadth of the village under cover. In the middle, surrounded by a wide moat still full of water, was the Rocca Sanvitale, an imposing brick castle originally built in the fifteenth century by the Sanvitale, one of the most illustrious and ancient families in Italy. The line is now extinct but at the time we arrived they had lived in the castle for some five hundred years. They lived a reclusive life and were hardly ever seen. The only one of them who appeared in public from time to time was the Conte's daughter, who was already past what was considered a marriageable age. She was tall and thin and extremely pale, with a very sad smile, and the only reason she crossed the moat to the village was to attend Mass. The Fontanellatesi called her *la Contessina ammuffita*, the musty princess.

Behind its moat and curtain walls the castle had a small garden with a turret at each end of it. In one of these turrets was a *camera oscura*, a dark room with a crystal prism set in it, which enabled the old Contessa to see the people walking in the square below. She must also have had good sources of information, as she was said to know all the gossip of the village.

Opposite the castle were the disused stables, which led into a beautifully romantic but neglected garden. And in the same square stood the parish church of Santa Croce, built at about the same time as the castle. It was a rather severe, red-brick, Gothic building on the outside but its interior was more pleasing; and like other churches it was patronized mainly by women and children. On the whole, the men of Fontanellato went to church only for feast days, funerals, christenings and weddings, or to ask some special favour of the Almighty.

Most of the houses in the village were quite large, with shutters which were only opened for a few hours in the mornings; if there was a breeze long lace curtains could be seen gently moving. At either end of the village two long avenues of trees gave it a friendly air. In warm weather you could sit in their shade on one of the numerous benches provided by the *municipio*. At the end of one of the avenues stood the Santuario della Madonna del Rosario, a large seventeenth-century church which was a famous place of pilgrimage. The Madonna and Child, whose wooden effigies were carved in 1615, were said to have put an end to the great plague of 1634-41 and to have performed other miracles ever since, and they attracted a constant stream of worshippers throughout the year. Inside, the church's walls were covered with *ex voto* offerings: primitive paintings portraying the incidents that gave rise to the various miracles – children falling into mill-races, ox-carts overturning, aeroplanes crashing. Then there were silver hearts, wooden legs, waxen hands, crutches, steering wheels from wrecked motor cars and many other objects, including framed photographs and letters of thanks. The Madonna presided over it all, high and serene above the altar, dressed in pale-blue silk embellished with golden embroidery.

The Santuario was looked after by Dominican monks, and they were a pretty shrewd lot when it came to business. Apart from collecting money from the offertory at Mass, which was always very well attended, they had a good income from what they charged individuals to have Masses said for the souls of the dead. They also sold souvenirs and, in exchange for suitably generous donations, gave out small, square pieces of the Virgin's dress. I never understood where all these squares of material came from because the demand was enormous; to meet it the Madonna's dress would have had to be changed almost every week. A body of Dominican nuns lived next door to the Santuario in the deepest seclusion, and participated in the Masses hidden from view behind bars.

The feasts of the Madonna fell on 15 August and 8 September, and on those days hundreds if not thousands of pilgrims decended on Fontanellato from all over the province and even further afield. They came on foot, in horse-drawn carts, by bicycle and by bus, arriving early in the morning so as to have a full day's prayer. Some approached the Santuario on their knees for the last part of the journey, saying the Rosary and imploring the Madonna's help.

Standing back from the main road, surrounded by green grass, was the memorial to those men of the village and the surrounding hamlets who had died during the Great War, and behind the memorial was the primary school which I was going to join in the course of the next few days.

Our home was much smaller than the house in Štanjel, which by comparison seemed a palace. Home now consisted of only two rooms and a kitchen, but fortunately we were allowed half of the attractive garden as well. This made my mother happy, as gardening and flowers were her great passion; it almost amounted to a vice.

In spite of the garden we took some time to get accustomed to our new way of living. We felt a little like prisoners and missed our privacy and independence; my mother was the most aware of this feeling as she was the one who was most at home.

The new school term was about to start and I felt very nervous. I knew nobody and had no idea of what to expect when I presented myself to the new teacher in my new black overall and white collar. She was a rather old lady, all dressed in black, with her white hair in a bun. Her name was Signora Puglia. She met me with a friendly smile, shook my hand and introduced me to the class: 'This is Wanda, our new pupil who has come to live in our village. She doesn't know anybody, so please be kind to her and I am sure you will become good friends.' Every eye was fixed on the new foreign girl, and then there was a clapping of hands. My face was as red as a tomato as I was shown to my seat.

Once the lessons began I realized that I was not nearly up to the standard of the others. The Italian the other children spoke in school was not a dialect like my Triestino and in many subjects I was in any case behind the others, a thought which made me very unhappy. That first day at school depressed me, and during the next few days I begged my parents to let me stay at home, which of course was out of the question. Signora Puglia was consulted and she suggested that she should give me private lessons after school to bring me up to the standard of the others. Soon I began to improve and my Triestino became proper Italian. Signora Puglia was convinced that with more lessons I could take the examination for the higher school in Parma, the Scuola Media. A year after I arrived in Fontanellato I did so and won a scholarship which paid half my school fees. During this year my father too succeeded in overcoming his difficulties with the language and with his new pupils. His problems had been much more serious than mine, but before long he was accepted by everyone.

During that first year in Fontanellato I was obliged to join the most junior of the Fascist organizations and became a *Piccola Italiana*, a little Italian. This meant that on special occasions I had to wear a black pleated skirt, white blouse and black beret, with white socks and black shoes and, when the weather was cold, a black cloak. At twelve I would become a *Giovane Italiana*, and at eighteen a *Giovane Fascista*. If you didn't join one of these organizations you couldn't go to school.

Fascism was not thought of as a separate subject on the school curriculum, but the history of how Mussolini came to power was dealt with at length at the end of the modern history text-books. We learned Fascist songs, and at the end of each term we would hold a gymnastic display for the Fascist authorities and our parents. On days of national holiday we had a parade, marching up and down and singing patriotic songs. I found it all very boring, especially when I got older, but kept my thoughts to myself.

Once the exams were over I had the whole summer free in front of me and a host of new friends to pass it with – the idea made me extremely happy. Fontanellato was very different from Štanjel. There were no real woods and no trenches to bomb; only lines of poplars and the endless rows of vines which separated the enormous cultivated fields from one another and broke the endless monotony of the *pianura*. Nevertheless, I soon adapted to my new landscape.

The bicycle was, and still is, an essential feature of the flat plain; there couldn't have been a single family without one. My best friends, Ada, Nora and Nives, all had bicycles, which put me at a serious disadvantage. I could hardly follow them on their wanderings unless one or other of them was prepared to take me on her saddle while she stood upright pedalling. I didn't even know how to ride a bicycle, though as it happened I was soon forced to learn.

About a kilometre from our house there was a large field given over exclusively to melons and watermelons, which do well in the Po valley because of the heat. One afternoon, while the Fontanellatesi were having their siesta, Nora called for me on her bicycle. 'Wanda, come for a ride. I'll take you on my saddle.' It was an offer I couldn't refuse. When we were outside the house, where no one could hear us, she said: 'As nobody is out at this time I thought it would be nice to go to that field which is full of melons. I have a big bag with me – we'll pick some and have a *scorpacciata* [a bellyful].'

We rode off to the field which was bursting with beautiful yellow melons, my favourite sort. There was no one in sight so we carefully started to collect the ripest ones. We were both absorbed in our work when we heard angry cries: the owner of the field hurrying towards us armed with a big stick. Nora had seen him first and was already running for dear life, not caring about her bag or the bicycle. I panicked too, and without a moment's hesitation mounted the bicycle and tried to ride away on it. By a miracle I found I could do it: standing upright on the pedals and pedalling with all my might I reached the road, where Nora was waiting for me. 'You didn't tell me you could ride,' she said, rather irritated, as if I had been keeping a secret from her. But I hadn't known myself.

Back at home I didn't mention that I had barely escaped being branded as a melon thief; but now, having ridden a bicycle, I realized that I would not be happy until I possessed one of my own. For my most recent birthday Danica, my godmother, had given me a wristwatch, thinking that such a gift was the dream of every girl. In fact it didn't excite me at all. Seeing my disappointed expression, she said that if I didn't want the watch she would keep it herself and give my mother money instead to buy something I would really like. That was how I eventually got my bicycle.

The money Danica gave my mother was not enough to buy one of the better sorts of bicycle, but it was no good buying a cheap one as it would have to last me for years. 'We will go to Tonino,' my mother said. It was fortunate that there was such a man as Tonino in Fontanellato. He was a good mechanic who specialized in collecting second-hand parts of bicycles and putting together strong, good-looking ones which were as shiny as new.

When my mother and I called on him he said that if we could wait a few days he would find the right frame and have it stove-enamelled black. With nickel-plated handlebars, new pedals, a new saddle, a basket to carry things in and a brightly coloured net over the rear wheel to stop my skirt getting tangled in the chain, the finished bicycle would look brand new. Tonino was proud of his work. He kept his promise and in a couple of weeks my beautiful, shiny bicycle was ready. I couldn't have been happier: there was nothing else I could wish for.

My father, my mother and I were often asked to spend Sunday afternoons in the country, but sometimes, unless a horse and cart were sent to collect us, we could not go because the families who invited us lived too far away. My father and I could have cycled, but my mother had never learnt. Finally I succeeded in persuading her to try. 'But who is going to teach me?' she asked. 'I will,' I said. 'It really isn't difficult. You sit on the saddle and try and keep your balance and hold on to the handlebars. There's no danger. I'll have one hand on the saddle and the other on the handlebars.'

I explained that in case of emergency she could easily touch the ground with her feet and, so encouraged, she came out with me to learn. What I hadn't considered was that she was much bigger than me and that I wasn't strong enough to keep both her and the bicycle upright: inevitably she lost her balance and fell heavily on the road with me and the bicycle on top of her. She escaped with some bruises but was adamant that she would never take lessons from me again. Eventually she learned to ride with the help of a neighbour.

The summer promised to be delicious, but nothing is ever perfect. My mother, not believing in idleness and thinking of the long months that lay ahead of me, decided I should learn embroidery. It was an art which did not excite me at all, but there was no way out.

In Fontanellato, as in many other villages in Italy, there were professional embroiderers who made a living by embroidering sheets, tablecloths, and nightdresses for brides' trousseaux, and also taught a few girls their skills for a small fee. I was to be one of these victims, and I had to go afternoon after hot afternoon to learn to embroider in a room that even with the windows open was almost completely airless, trying to keep my eyes open while I stitched and listened to endless gossip. It was from my teacher and her two other pupils, who were older than me, that I learnt about all the intrigues and scandals that went on in the village.

After a few hours of embroidery I was free; free to cycle wherever I liked with my friends. We often went to the house of Don Cattabianchi, the priest of Santa Croce, a very eccentric but equally intelligent and learned man. His house was a primitive version of a modern youth club. We played various games there, of which the most popular was a kind of bingo. We had long discussions about whatever we liked, and during term-time Don Cattabianchi would sometimes help us with our homework. If he was at home we were always welcome in his study. Other rooms, especially the kitchen, could only be entered by special permission from his rather fat, one-legged sister, who acted as his *perpetua* or housekeeper. When I was a little older I enjoyed going there because I was sure of meeting some of the boys I liked, but on these matters Don Cattabianchi was very strict. In order to keep the boys separate from the girls he used to draw a chalk line down the middle of our meeting room, and when we got carried away and crossed the line he would burst into a ferocious rage, pick up anything that was to hand – usually a book – and throw it at the offender, who had to duck fast in order not to be hit.

If any one of his rules was broken – and he had a number – he would put a notice on his front door which said that the offender was *scartata*, rejected; it could be for a few days or anything up to a fortnight. Sometimes when there were a lot of us, he would open the church hall, and there, if things went wrong, he would exercise his sudden outbursts of temper even more ferociously. He would even throw chairs, and when this happened we quickly made for the exit. I never understood why he had such fits of fury because normally he was the kindest and most considerate of men. Was it the moon that influenced him? It is widely believed in Italy that the moon has a great influence on human beings and on nature. The farmers never sow their seeds without consulting the calendar which shows the phases of the moon. It is the same in Slovenia.

Every spring he would hire a small bus to take the older children to the foothills of the Apennines. We were always the guests of some local parish priest, and our outings were great fun as we were allowed to run more or less wild once we had arrived. One expedition, however, did not go according to plan. The postal service was rather vague in these remote villages, and perhaps a letter had gone astray, for when we arrived at what we thought would be our host's house, we found that the old *perpetua* did not know we were coming. She told us that the priest would not be back until the afternoon.

Disappointed but not beaten, Don Cattabianchi said, 'We can't wait here for hours. We'll go for a walk in the hills and for lunch we will go and have some sandwiches in a *trattoria*.' We all felt happy about this and began to walk towards a distant wood, but as we approached it we saw two figures emerging: the priest we had come to see arm in arm with an attractive girl. It was an embarrassing situation, more so for them than for us. The two priests greeted each other rather coldly and we carried on with our walk. The incident was never mentioned again.

Don Cattabianchi's wish was that when he died there should be a big party in the church hall, with singing and dancing and no dividing line down the middle of the floor, but unfortunately this was not to be. After years in Fontanellato he was moved by the Bishop, for reasons no one knew at the time, to a lonely parish in the foothills of the Apennines above Parma, where life was not nearly so pleasant for him. He became very withdrawn and died there not long afterwards.

Many years later I learned that the Bishop, whose sympathies were with the Fascists, had sent Don Cattabianchi to this distant parish because of the priest's opposition to the regime. During his last year in Fontanellato Don Cattabianchi had been woken up in the night on a number of occasions and beaten by the secret police. Nobody had known about it at the time.

On summer afternoons the streets of Fontanellato were almost completely deserted. This was the time when everyone had a siesta and for a few hours the village was virtually dead. The doors of the houses were closed and the shutters left open just enough to allow some fresh air to penetrate the rooms. Even the flies were silent.

Apart from the very young, who were not interested in having siestas, the only human beings to be seen were a few women who preferred to sit in the shade of their houses. They passed the time chatting as they knitted or mended. If I did have a siesta it was always a very short one. Usually I took my bicycle and went off in search of friends who, like me, were too full of energy to want to rest. 'Go home, dear girl, you will die of heat on your bicycle,' the women under the arcades would say to me in their strange Parmigiano dialect (which I soon learned to understand but never to speak) as I rode past. Out in the open the heat was intense. The plain shimmered below a cloudless sky, and it was not unusual to hear that some *contadino* (peasant) who had been working in the afternoon heat had been taken to the local hospital suffering or even dying from sunstroke.

At night, after those incandescent afternoons, the sky was deep blue and filled with stars, which in August began to shoot in great arcs across the sky. It was difficult to sleep. The sheets seemed as heavy as blankets and Flit was the only thing that prevented the mosquitoes descending on us like vultures. In summer the smell of Flit was always with us. Apparently no one ever thought of using mosquito nets.

After the siesta, shops began to open and normal rhythms were resumed. Fontanellato was at its liveliest towards dusk. Men sat outside the cafés discussing business, chatting or playing *briscola*, a card game, as they sipped glasses of *lambrusco*, while we young girls walked up and down the main street and through the square on what was called the *passeggiata*, the promenade, hoping that we attracted the eyes of the boys who gathered in little groups. We were all very young and shy and none of us had the courage to approach and speak to them.

On Sunday afternoons, because our parents would not let us go out unaccompanied in the evenings, we used to go to the local cinema, which was also the theatre. A small, elegant building, it had been constructed in the last century by the Sanvitale family, who had always been passionate lovers of music and theatre.

My parents could only afford to give me some small change on Sundays, but it was enough for a cinema ticket and an ice cream. Very often the film, which was always very old and fragile, broke; and usually at the most exciting part. When this happened we had to wait until it was repaired, and if it proved impossible we were entitled to see the next film, the following Sunday, for nothing. Many of the films were silent, but the people who went to the evening performances could enjoy a musical accompaniment played on the piano by the local music teacher, who was blind.

In Fontanellato there was one old woman who was a hunchback, and she lived alone in a rather dark, spooky flat. We called her *la strega*, the witch. She was supposed to have the power of healing stomach aches, and people used to visit her during the hours of the siesta so that no one would know. I went once with my mother because I was curious to know how the old woman exercised her magic. She held one end of a white tape in one hand and measured out a length with the other which was several times the distance from her elbow to the second finger of her hand. Then she asked the 'patient' to hold the other end while she measured out the length again, mumbling a strange, unintelligible gibberish all the while. If the second measurement did not tally exactly with the first, it meant that there was something wrong with the patient's stomach. She repeated the exercise several times until she got two identical measurements and then the customer went home, satisfied and cured. Before she died *la strega* left her secrets to Signora Grignaffini, our landlady, who looked a bit like a witch herself.

One regular visitor to *la strega*, and later to Signora Grignaffini, was Amelia. She was a strange, skinny woman always dressed in dark clothes, and her face looked as if it had never seen the sun. She was housekeeper to a *nano*, a dwarf, called Appio who was always dressed in a suit with baggy trousers which made his rather stout figure look even broader. The rumour was that Amelia was not as frail as she looked. When Appio did not listen to her she would get angry, lift him like a feather and set him on top of a chest of drawers. He would be left there, unable to get down without help, until he apologized and did as she said.

Not far from where we lived was the local hospital, the Ospedale Peracchi. It was sometimes used for emergencies but it was mainly a hospital for old people. It was run by a very good and able nun, Mother Superior Eusebia, or Suor Eusebia as she was commonly known, with the help of three other nuns. There was also an *infermiere*, a male nurse, named Luigi who looked like a retired boxer. Luigi was also the dentist's assistant, and he was often called upon to perform urgent extractions himself, as the dentist only held a surgery once a week. He would put on a white overall for the occasion, more to impress the customer than for hygienic reasons, then have a good look at the tooth. Without a word he would get hold of it with his forceps and proceed to extract it without anaesthetic, exclaiming with great satisfaction, '*Via il dente, via il dolore*', 'Tooth gone, pain gone'. As a finale he would wipe off the blood and put a great chunk of disinfected cotton wool in the patient's mouth.

Luigi did not charge very much for this operation, and if the patient was poor he did it for nothing. He was either very lucky or very skilful, because although his techniques were primitive no one ever seemed to suffer from any complications. No one ever had a chance to change his or her mind, either. Once you were in the chair the tooth was as good as out, because Luigi had no intention of missing a chance to exercise his skill. He just loved the idea of being a dentist.

As September drew on, the days grew cooler. Knowing that I had to start at a new school in the city, with new people and new teachers, I began to worry all over again. For me a town was a mysterious, rather forbidding place and I was afraid that I would feel very much alone. I was to travel the seventeen kilometres to Parma every day in a tram which was hauled by a steam engine. It left at half past seven, which meant getting up soon after half past six, and the journey took about an hour. There were only two coaches which for the most part were filled with students – except on Parma's market days, Wednesdays and Saturdays, when they were crowded with country people. Saturdays made no difference to us, for there was no school then, but on Wednesdays some of us had to stand up the whole way to Parma.

The morning journey, in spite of the number of students on board the tram, was usually quiet. Almost all of us were trying to catch up on our homework, although the tram was much too bumpy for anyone to write anything. The journey back in the late afternoon was completely different, noisy and ringing with laughter. It was the happiest time of the day: lessons were over and the long written homework could not be started. At Ponte Taro the tram divided; two cars went to Medesano, and two to Fontanellato and Busseto. Part of the ritual of returning home was hearing the loud injunction to passengers to remind them to change if necessary: 'Fontanellato, Soragna, Busseto, Noceto, Medesano, *si cambia!*'

Once a fortnight a very severe-looking lawyer, an *avvocato*, used to travel to Parma on the tram. He had white hair and a white moustache and was dressed in a dark suit and stiff white collar. He always sat at the end of the second coach, in the small, first-class compartment with red plush seats. He was the only person I ever saw using it, and I suspect it was especially dusted for his benefit; the rest of the tram was tremendously dusty all summer. The lawyer never spoke to anyone, never smiled and never lifted his eyes from the innumerable papers he seemed to be reading through his monocle.

The driver of the tram was an enormous man. He wore a black uniform with a black cap and had a very black face due to the coal dust which rose in clouds when he shovelled coal into the engine. Only his bright red lips and large blue eyes stood out from the general blackness. He spoke very little and we hardly knew him because he was up in front with the engine. We didn't even know his name, so we called him Carnera, after the Italian heavyweight-boxing champion, Primo Carnera. He was very well disposed towards his student passengers. About three kilometres before he reached Fontanellato each morning he began to sound the whistle on the engine to warn us that he would soon be arriving. If one of us was really late, but could be seen running to catch the tram, Carnera waited, even if it meant starting a little behind time. His next stop was Fontevivo, then Bellena, where a rather handsome air-force pilot used sometimes to get on. (He was courting a friend and fellow student of mine, and used to fly low over the village and perform aerobatics to show his love for her until he got into trouble for it.)

After it had crossed the Torrente Taro the tram had a dead straight journey for the rest of the way, stopping at three more places and picking up just a few more passengers, none of whom were regulars. How it could have been made to pay is a mystery. Except in winter, when heavy snow sometimes delayed us and another engine had to come to the rescue, we generally arrived on time at Parma. Just occasionally a tram car went off the rails; perhaps Carnera was overcome by the thrill of speed. In summer this was heaven for us because it sometimes took hours to put things right and we would miss a large chunk of lessons. In winter it was hell. It might have been difficult for the headmaster of our school to believe that we were late because of a derailment, but fortunately a teacher of theology at the school, Don Cavalli, travelled on the tram every day, and he was able to explain what had happened, giving us a cast-iron alibi.

The tram journey, although long and monotonous, was usually fun, but in winter the compartments were bitterly cold. We had *scaldini* – large, flat, iron containers which were filled with hot water at the outset of each journey – to put our feet on. Without them we would have arrived in Parma absolutely frozen. There were just three *scaldini* in each compartment, so most of the time we had to take turns. Sometimes they were so hot that they burned the soles of our shoes. But their biggest drawback was that they caused chilblains. My feet were sometimes so painful and swollen that I could only walk with my heels out of my shoes. My hands got very cold too, but my mother helped me every morning by baking two potatoes in their skins for me to keep in my pockets; they retained their heat for quite a long time. During all the years I went to school in Parma she never failed to get up to warm the kitchen and give me hot drinks, however early it had to be; it was sometimes five o'clock, if I had to finish work from the night before.

On my first day at the Istituto Tecnico Macedonio Melloni, which was about twenty minutes' walk from where the tram stopped, all the new pupils were being greeted at the top of a large staircase by the headmaster, a rather forbidding figure who had a white beard and gold-rimmed spectacles, and was dressed in a black suit.

Then we were shown the locker room, which had a section for each class. In my own section, towards the middle of the cloakroom, I saw to my horror two lines of girls staring at me and giggling, and as I came near, one of them asked in a sarcastic voice where I came from. These were my future classmates, and my relationship with them depended on how I reacted now. If I showed shyness or fear my life would be a misery. I took courage, stopped, looked my questioner straight in the eye and said, 'I come from Fontanellato by tram and I am here for the same reason as you are. Any other questions?' These girls were all Parmigiane who knew each other. They thought they could make fun of a country

83

girl, but my answer took them by surprise. After this confrontation they were quite kind, and in time we became good friends.

On that first day I had little thought to spare for Parma itself, but gradually I came to realize how fortunate I was to go to school in a city that was both beautiful and intensely interesting. Parma grew on me as the years passed. I slowly began to understand its sophistication and culture and the Parmigiani's enthusiasm for life and good food. Stendhal immortalized the city in *La Chartreuse de Parme*, describing the beautiful women who walked in the streets as Madonnas who had just emerged from the paintings of Correggio and Parmigianino. Correggio was born in Reggio Emilia, forty kilometres from Parma, and Parmigianino in Parma itself.

The city's best season was the autumn, when the leaves were turning and it was filled with a soft golden light which earned it the name of Aurea Parma. It was divided into two distinct parts by the Torrente Parma. A *torrente* is a river which usually flows only after rain or the melting of the snows; most of the rivers that descend from the Apennines towards the Po and the Adriatic are *torrenti*, more or less dry in summer except for an occasional pool where you could swim in those far-off days without much danger to your health.

On the west side of the *torrente* was Parma Vecchia, old Parma, otherwise known to the local inhabitants as Oltre Torrente (Beyond the Torrent) or, in the dialect, Di là dell'Acqua. The inhabitants of Di là dell'Acqua formed a very individual community, smaller but very much like that of London East Enders before the war. They were generally poorer than those on the east bank of the *torrente*, where the principal monuments were, and almost all of them were Communists. In 1922 Parma became the last city in Italy to give in to Mussolini, and then only after violent fighting *Oltre Torrente*.

Out in the country, too, in places like Fontanellato, most of the *contadini* were Communist. When they went on strike against the landlords in 1908, blood flowed in Parma. The Communism in Parma bore, and still bears, very little resemblance to the Communism in other parts of Europe; in fact it was different from that of Bologna, which is only about eighty kilometres away down the Via Emilia. After the Second World War this countryside witnessed the struggle between the priests and embryo commissars described in Guareschi's *Don Camillo*, a struggle which continued, in a more mild form, until comparatively recently.

Parma became renowned for its elegance during the reign of Maria Luigia, Napoleon's second wife, daughter of the Emperor of Austria and mother of the King of Rome, when she was Duchess of Parma, Piacenza and Guastalla; although it had already been famous under the Farnese and the Bourbons. It was Maria Luigia who commissioned the building of the Teatro Regio, with its white and gold and red plush interior, and appointed Paganini, who had lived in Parma since the age of twelve, to be one of the directors of her orchestra, at that time the finest in all Italy.

I soon discovered that opera was a passion for the Parmigiani, who had extremely critical ears. The boys in my class would come to school during the opera season, which was always in the winter, and discuss the previous night's performance at every opportunity. They queued for hours in order to secure the cheapest standing places in the *loggioni*, the back part of the gallery. There was a better than fifty-fifty chance that the opera would be one by Verdi, who was born near Busseto.

It was the listeners up in the *loggioni* of whom the singers were most afraid: if the performance did not reach a sufficiently high standard in the opinion of the audience, the most vocal members of which were in the *loggioni*, they would be treated to *il fischio*, an outburst of whistling accompanied by the stamping of feet and sometimes a barrage of tomatoes or fruit. But if the performance was good the ovations had no limit, the audience felt happy for days, and the *Gazetta di Parma*, Italy's second oldest newspaper, ran columns of praise.

Maria Luigia also extended the Palatine Library, which had been founded by Philip of Bourbon, Duke of Parma, and contained a complete collection of the works printed by the press of Giambattista Bodoni together with the original typefaces. She commissioned the building of the Convitto Maria Luigia, once a school for boys which could almost have been described as the Eton of Italy. She built one palace in Parma and another, a sort of miniature Versailles, not far from the Po at Colorno, which later became a lunatic asylum.

The women of Parma were very elegant. They had a passion for clothes, and every particular of how a dress or coat was made was studied in the most minute detail. This was largely due to the fact that the Duchess brought her ladies-in-waiting from Paris with her when she came to Parma. Furniture and furnishings in Parma show a strong French influence, too, being Parmesan adaptations of the Empire style; and the local dialect has numerous words which are purely French (although these must have been imported at an earlier time, perhaps under the Bourbons in the eighteenth century) – *armoir* for *armadio* (a wardrobe), *vin* for *vino*, *bouchon* for *tappo* (a cork), *artichaut* for *carciofo* (an artichoke), and so on. The father of a friend of mine who went to visit relatives in Paris told us that he did not know a word of French but spoke the Parmigiano dialect all the time and got on very well.

The heart of that part of Parma that was not Oltre Torrente was Piazza Garibaldi, which was bisected by the Via Emilia on its way from Milan to Rimini. In the spring and autumn – not so much in the summer because the heat drove the better-off inhabitants into the foothills – the Piazza assumed a joyous aspect. The cavernous cafés and the tables outside were full of people, old and young, sipping coffee or aperitifs, or enjoying a *coppa*, a glass full of delicious ice cream. (A *coppa* was my favourite treat but unfortunately I could not afford it very often.) There was a clock on the tower of the Governor's Palace which overlooked the square (and a sundial which gave the time in Agra, Tobolsk, Isfahan and Moscow in the mornings and in Lima, Buenos Aires, Pico di Teneriffe, Lisbon, Paris and Rio in the afternoons). As soon as the offices and shops closed at noon, the square and all the streets leading off it were filled with bicycles, then as now the best way of getting about in Parma. Girls could be seen riding slowly past with one hand on the handlebars, the other full of books which they were taking home after the morning's lessons. Meanwhile the boys stood on the pavements with their bicycles nearby, admiring the girls and commenting on their looks; greetings to friends rang out on all sides.

On Wednesday mornings the Piazza Garibaldi took on a completely different aspect: it was monopolized from an early hour by farmers who came to town to sell their livestock in the Mercato del Bestiame on the outskirts of the city. There sellers and buyers, sometimes after hours of negotiations with the aid of the *mediatore* – men like Signor Grignaffini, who well knew the value of the *bestiame* in question – would eventually agree on a price.

In winter most of the farmers wore *tabarri*, and felt hats made by Borsalino or Panizza, two well-known Italian hat-makers; they were a bit like the sort of hat worn by Al Capone. Buyers and sellers stood immobile in the freezing Piazza: they looked sinister and almost inanimate until they left their posts for coffee or hot punch in one of the cafés.

Late afternoon before the shops closed, winter and summer, was the time for the *passeggiata*. Women and girls would appear in droves, dressed in their carefully planned outfits, to promenade slowly past the smart Caffè Bizzi, a beautiful shiny place like an Aladdin's Cave, of a sort that is now almost extinct in Italy. Some of the older women might stop for an *aperitivo* after window-shopping in Via Cavour, which led into the Piazza. This was the time known as *sull'imbrunire*, when the sky was still bright in the west and the clock on the Governor's Palace was lit up.

I did not often take part in the *passeggiata* because soon after school ended I had to go home on the tram, but sometimes a schoolfriend of mine called Wilma used to invite me to stay the night if there was a lot of homework to be done.

This was a big treat for me. As soon as school was finished we used to rush back to her house and start on our homework immediately, so as to have an hour or so for the *passeggiata* before going back for supper and finishing off. On one occasion a boy I rather liked looked at me and said to his group, '*Bellezza d'asino*' (beauty of a donkey), which, strange as it may seem, was meant in Parma as a compliment. It was a compliment with a sting though, because it implied that this was a kind of good looks that would not last.

Another time, Wilma's parents took us both to the Teatro Regio to see *La Traviata*, my first opera, and I had a new dress for the occasion. It took me for ever to decide on the colour, style and material it was to be made in. Eventually, as I was very blonde, I chose a soft brown wool material embroidered with chenille of the same colour. I will never forget entering the brilliantly lit theatre, gilded and hung with great chandeliers, and seeing the women in ethereally lovely dresses. It was a world beyond my wildest dreams; one I had only seen on celluloid in the cinema at Fontanellato.

At that time almost no one bought ready-made dresses in

88

Italy. Every town and village had its dressmakers, and even pullovers were usually made locally, knitted to order on machines. But sometimes, when I had time to spare, I used to look for a bargain in the Mercato della Ghiaia, the Gravel Market, which still exists today. It sold a wonderful variety of *salumi* and cheese (principally *grana*, *formaggio Parmigiano*), shoes, agricultural instruments and materials, some of them at much reduced prices. A friend of mine called Nelia, who travelled with me on the tram to Parma each day, used to visit the market quite often. I never understood why until one morning I saw her in a corner sobbing.

'Nelia, what's happened?' I asked. 'Why are you crying?'

'Please go away, and don't ask any questions,' she said. 'I'd rather be left alone.' But she was obviously very upset and I felt I couldn't leave her. Eventually she explained that she owed money to a stall-keeper who sold second-hand clothing: she had stupidly borrowed some from him to buy a dress. Now he was insisting that she should give him the dress she was wearing to pay off the debt. 'How can I go to school in nothing but my underwear?' she asked in tears. Eventually, together, we persuaded the man that Nelia should pay what she owed in instalments.

I studied at the Scuole Medie in the Istituto Melloni, which would enable me, after four years, to choose either a classical or a scientific education by taking the appropriate examination. In my class there were more boys than girls. Our teacher for the main subjects, Italian, Latin, History and Geography, was an elderly spinster who, under a kindly face, was very tough. Although she had pronounced likes and dislikes for the various members of her class she was perhaps the best teacher in the school, and at the end of four years she had hardly any failures in the final examinations.

For all the eight years I attended school in Parma there was always the problem of where to eat the midday meal –

at that time no school in Italy provided lunches. When I first arrived, at the age of twelve, I was advised to try a family in Borgo delle Colonne, a long cobbled street with an arcade along one side, very typical of Parma, where a woman who ran a small dairy business undertook to look after me. Her husband appeared very seldom. He worked outside the city, and was sometimes away for days at a time.

While I was having lunch soldiers from the local garrison used to come in for snacks. All of them seemed to be on rather intimate terms with the proprietress, who was a very handsome, dark-haired woman, tall and well-built, with penetrating eyes. I had only recently heard of the existence of such places, but I gradually came to the conclusion that she was running a small brothel of which she herself was the centre of interest. I had no proof of it but I was much too shy to eat every day in the company of soldiers anyway, so I decided to find somewhere else to eat. That part of Parma, around Borgo delle Colonne, was apparently well known for its brothels, and I often used to see heavily made-up women in tight skirts and high-heeled shoes decorated with silver stars parading up and down; I assume now that they were what the Parmigiani used to refer to as *putane*, whores.

My second lunch place was on the fifth floor of a house in the same road as the school, the Via Farini. I liked it because it was a corner flat and from one of the windows I could look down into Piazza Garibaldi. The lady who took me in was a widow with a son of about my age who hardly ever spoke. She was an attractive, red-haired woman, but she looked sad and always dressed in black out of respect for her dead husband. The atmosphere was not exactly lively but I continued to have lunch there for a long time because she was extremely kind and the food was good. She told me that just across the road there lived what she described as a *mantenuta*, a kept woman, whose lover visited her every day: she could be seen waiting for him behind the semi-closed shutters.

Besides looking expensively elegant, which is what I expected a *mantenuta* to be, this woman was also very beautiful. I used to look at her and admire her but I also felt sorry for her because she was always confined to the flat. The widow told me that she went out twice a day – once very early for shopping and once for a walk towards evening – but never where the *passeggiata* took place.

I eventually got tired of the sad lady and the *mantenuta* and started once again to look for something different. I found a *pensione* on the first floor of a small square, run by a woman so enormous that she could hardly move. As well as giving me lunch, she had rooms to let which were permanently occupied by her 'regulars'; two lawyers, a mature medical student and a businessman. I was accepted as part of the family, which consisted of two daughters and a grandfather; the husband had died many years before. The food was excellent and I was not charged much because the cooking was done on quite a large scale – I was not a big eater so my lunch did not make much difference to the running of the place. I soon discovered that if someone arrived late all the remains of the plates of pasta were put together and presented to him or her. From that day I ate only pasta dressed with butter and felt safe, because I knew that however late I arrived it would have been saved for me; no one else would eat it plain.

The *pensione* suited me. If for any reason I had to spend the night in town and my friend Wilma couldn't have me, I could stay there very cheaply with the girls. The paying guests kept very much to themselves. When they had eaten their lunch in the dining room they withdrew to their rooms for a siesta. But I noticed that at times the fat proprietress went to their rooms; to play cards, she said. From time to time new temporary guests appeared. Some of them were younger and jollier than their predecessors, and enjoyed a little dancing to the music of a gramophone. I was invited to join in but always found excuses not to do so, saying that I had early afternoon lessons. This was not because I didn't want to dance but because I had not yet learned how to do it properly.

So I went out, feeling distinctly lonely, and wandered through the empty, narrow streets of lunch-time Parma until the time really came to go back to school. One afternoon, as I walked under the tall arches of the Palazzo della Pilotta, the immense, pale-pink building constructed in the time of the Farnese with millions of thin bricks, a fat middle-aged man exposed himself to me. It was at this moment that I decided I must learn to dance, so that I could stay on at the *pensione* instead of roaming about.

It was not difficult to learn if you wanted to. Every Sunday in the country a different village had what was called a *balera*, a large marquee with a highly polished wooden floor and a small orchestra which played all afternoon and evening, with an interval for supper. It was cheaper than the cinema, only a few pennies, and young people could sometimes get in for nothing if they attached themselves to an adult. I soon learned to dance, beginning with other girls as partners.

I must have been about fifteen when I received my first love letter. It was delivered very secretly by a student of the Convitto Maria Luigia who travelled on the tram, and it had been given to him by another boy at the same school, a boarder whom I knew well and who lived in Fontenallato. He was called Paolo, and he was a handsome, elegant, *simpatico* boy whom I often saw and talked to during the school holidays, without ever suspecting that he was interested in me personally. Now he was saying that although we were too young to talk of real love he hoped we would see each other alone and not always surrounded by friends. I didn't answer the letter, but just counted the days and the hours until he would be home for the holidays; they seemed interminable. I could not concentrate on anything. I just daydreamed and felt intensely happy.

When he came home we saw each other often. We would meet in the *balera* and spend the whole afternoon dancing together. My mother, having strict ideas about morality, would never allow me to go to *balere* in the evenings, so we spent them sitting on a wall near our house, usually with other friends. I didn't want my parents to know I had a boyfriend: they would not have approved because they would have felt I was too young.

As spring came and the evenings became warmer, the boys began to serenade the girls at night with songs, accompanying themselves on a guitar or mandolin. They played in the darkest part of the street where they could not be seen, but it was not difficult to guess who they were. I kept my window wide open to encourage them but my mother had different ideas. A few times she shouted at them, saying that they were disturbing the peace of the neighbourhood, but this did not discourage them; a few evenings later they would come back with new songs.

These were wonderful years in my life. I was young, I had no worries, I was in love. Even the nights were happy, full of wonderful dreams which almost amounted to a second life. Some of them were less pleasant, but fortunately these were rare. Like my mother, and many other people from Slovenia, I occasionally had dreams of premonition. The one I most clearly remember presaged the unfortunate end of a middle-aged unmarried woman who lived opposite us: I saw ropes and dark rooms and finally this woman hanging from a ceiling. I woke up screaming with terror and distress, and told my mother of the dream. The next day the news was all over

Fontanellato that the woman had been found dead with a rope round her neck.

The *festa* we all looked forward to in the village was that of the miraculous Madonna on 15 August. Three or four days before, a circus and a funfair with electric dodgem cars, slides and sideshows were set up. Then, early on 14 August, stalls selling souvenirs, all kinds of religious objects, sweets, primitive toys, salamis and cheese would spring up in the approaches to the Santuario.

A man and his wife positioned themselves in the middle of one of the tree-lined avenues and sang ballads to a harmonica. Most of them dealt with love and passion and violent death, and the subjects were already well known to the crowds from newspaper reports. Each song was repeated a number of times until the audience had learned the tune, then copies of it were offered for sale. These were always printed on paper of a lurid colour – a different colour for each song – and illustrated with crude drawings of the events described. I don't know who composed the ballads, which could be heard sung in the streets all over the place. I only know that I was never allowed to sing them at home. They were not all scandalous, though; some were conventional love songs of the sort you could hear at the cinema or on the radio, if you had one.

The greatest event of the day was the lunch that every local family prepared. This started at about midday and went on until late afternoon, when everyone was so full of food that they could hardly move. For patron-saint days in the country the table was usually prepared out of doors, in the shade of a large tree. No one had a drink before the food arrived, but once it did the wine flowed freely: the best *lambrusco*, the best *fortana* and finally the *moscato*, a sweet, white, generally fizzy wine made with selected muscatel grapes.

94

We often began with *antipasto*: a selection of home-cured *salumi*. There was *culatello*, part of the pig's bottom – this was difficult to produce because it had to be carefully matured, and was correspondingly expensive. The best came from Zibello, a village near the Po and not far from Fontanellato. There was *coppa*, made from the muscular part of the pig's neck where it meets the shoulder, and *prosciutto*, Parma ham, which comes from the same part of the pig as English gammon, and is cured in specially air-cooled rooms up in the foothills of the Apennines above Parma.

After this there was a pause before the soup appeared. Invariably this was made of boiled capon or chicken and beef, thickened with a special sort of pasta called *tempestina* ('small hail') or home-made *tagliatelle*. Then came the *carne lessa*, the boiled meat which had provided the soup, with *salsa verde*, a delicious sauce made with finely chopped parsley, hard-boiled egg, capers, anchovies, oil and white bread soaked in vinegar.

Then there was a long interval and very lively conversation filled the time before the next course: a roast guinea fowl and chicken, wonderfully aromatic with masses of rosemary, golden potatoes cooked in the juice from the birds, and young green salad. I have never since tasted such delicious potatoes and salad.

Pudding was always the *bisulan*, or in pure Italian *ciambella*: a round cake the texture of shortbread, with a hole in the middle and sugar on top. The sweet wine which accompanied the *bisulan* was kept in sand under the stairs if there was no cellar. Lunch ended with fruits and nuts. By about six o'clock it would be finished and the *rezdore*, the housewives in the dialect, would clear the tables and do the washing-up, gossiping and laughing.

Throughout this gargantuan meal the talk was almost entirely concentrated on food, on remembering other great meals, or discussing the quality of the ham and the other *salumi*: 'It mustn't just be pink; it mustn't be too fat, and it should be cut so thin that you can almost see the church tower through it.'

Others would discuss the question of how many *agnolini*, small, stuffed pasta envelopes, a man could eat, or assess the quality of the wine. After lunch there was always an interval during which the men remained seated, perhaps leaning their heads on the table for a *pisolino*, a nap – exhausted after all the eating, drinking and argument.

Then, finally, came supper, which was really what was left over from lunch: cold meat, salad and cheese, and more wine. My parents and I generally got a lift home in a cart, leaving some of the other guests still in deep discussion and the small children asleep on their mothers' laps.

III

Rumours of War

I WAS TWELVE when people began talking about East Africa and a possible Italian invasion of Abyssinia. Italy had two small colonies, Eritrea and Somalia, on the borders of Haile Selassie's Empire, which Mussolini was looking for an excuse to invade. At that time, in 1934, Mussolini was at the height of his power and popularity. He was not only able to make most of his subjects feel proud of being Italians but also succeeded to a great extent in making them believe that his great dream of giving Italy an important place in the world, as important as that of Britain and France, could become a reality. Since the Risorgimento in the nineteenth century, when the movement for political unification had taken place, Italy had experienced hard times and many political humiliations, so in 1929, when Mussolini ended the friction between the Church and the State by signing a concordat with the Vatican, most people really believed that the country was destined for a great future.

Being in a position of absolute power, Mussolini did everything he could to ensure his continuing popularity by constructing *autostrade*, electrifying railways and making the trains run on time, as well as by such elaborate schemes as draining the Pontine Marshes, previously infested by malarial mosquitoes, and reclaiming them for agriculture. Because he wanted a stronger and healthier nation, for much the same reason as Hitler did, on the other side of the Alps – to turn the men into warriors and the women into the mothers of warriors – he started what were known as *colonie marine e montane*, to which needy children were sent on holiday. He also established La Festa dell'Uva, the Fête of the Grapes, to encourage people to eat more of them.

In March 1934 Mussolini began to talk about natural expansion and the ability of Italy to civilize Africa. It was then that the Italian people began to understand what his intentions were; and when he later referred to the need for the colonies to be protected from aggression, it seemed clear that war in Africa could not be avoided. There were people in Italy who felt that the country was ill-prepared for any sort of war: my father was one of them. He was still more worried about the extensive rewriting of history that school text-books had been subjected to; something of which most of us remained unaware until after the Second World War.

He was supported in his anti-Fascist beliefs by his great friend the local general practitioner, Dr Sambataro, who lived in Fontanellato. A tall, very intelligent, rather bear-like man, and a Sicilian by birth, the doctor was highly regarded by his colleagues and patients alike. Like my father he did not suffer fools gladly, and he had an air of considerable authority which belied his great kindness. Because of his standing in the village he ventured at times to talk in a way which later proved disastrous about his anti-Fascist feelings. He thought he would come to no harm both because people needed his services as a medical man and because he thought they would regard him as nothing more than a political eccentric. After school my father used to accompany him on his rounds in the car, and during these journeys they had ample time to exchange ideas without being overheard.

In October 1935, in spite of the treaty of friendship he had made with Abyssinia in 1928, Mussolini gave orders to the Italian army to invade. Italy had actually played a major part in getting Abyssinia admitted to the League of Nations in 1923, eleven years previously. When the invasion took place, the League imposed economic sanctions on Italy, but these were never strictly enforced: what could have been a decisive embargo, on the sale of oil to a country which was chronically short of it, was never implemented. Mussolini took advantage of these largely theoretical impositions to say that the League's intention was to destroy the Italian economy and, surprising as it may seem today, the people of Italy reinforced what proved to be his growing megalomania by demonstrating, when inspired to do so by the press, that they were ready to make any sacrifices that might be asked of them. Entire families gave the nation whatever precious metal they possessed, and married women exchanged their gold wedding rings for iron ones. The first to do so was the Queen of Italy. Some strong-minded women, however, of whom my mother was one, did not take kindly to being parted from their most precious possession. They gave up other rings and wore iron ones in public so that they could be seen to have done their duty, which was what really mattered.

The invasion of Abyssinia was carried out successfully with the aid of poison gas and the widespread payment of bribes to local chieftains. Italy moved from victory to victory. The announcement of the conquests of Adowa and Makalle was followed at home by demonstrations of support and enthusiasm, organized by supporters of the Fascist regime, for the most part older students. We all marched through the streets of Parma cheering and singing and carrying banners which displayed Mussolini's slogans and the names of the places conquered. Songs were written to celebrate the victories; some of them were offensive and most of them were absurd. One particularly stupid one ran as follows:

And with the beard of the Emperor
we will make little brushes
to shine the shoes
of Benito Mussolini.

But the most popular song of all was 'Faccetta Nera':

Little Black Face, beautiful Abyssinian,
wait and hope
because the hour is drawing near
when we shall be near you
we shall give you a different law
and a different king.

Because we knew that the headmaster of the Scuola Medie Inferiori, where I was now in my last year, was not in a position to punish us if we did not appear for lessons on demonstration days, many of us took part only for a short time and then went home. Otherwise, if the weather was good, we would spend the rest of the day with our friends among the marble busts and statues in the romantic Giardino Pubblico, which had once been the Parco Ducale of Maria Luigia's palace.

Mussolini was determined to put a quick end to the war. Ignoring the advice of General de Bono, the Commander-in-Chief, who wanted a pause in the advance in order to consolidate his gains and improve communications, he replaced him with General Badoglio. Badoglio lost no time in advancing on the capital, Addis Ababa – from which the Emperor, Haile Selassie, had already fled to Britain – and entered it triumphantly on 5 May 1936. Four days later the Duce, from the balcony of the Palazzo Venezia in Rome, proclaimed Italy an Empire and the King its Emperor. The crowds were delirious with joy and, according to Mussolini, he himself felt that this was the most triumphant day of his entire life. There were now huge pictures of him everywhere, and endless slogans which even to me, young and silly as I was, seemed completely mindless: *'Credere, Obbedire, Combattere'* ('Believe, Obey, Fight') and *'Se avanzo seguitemi, se indietreggio uccidetemi'* ('If I advance follow me, if I retreat kill me') were two of the more popular ones. They were painted on the walls of many private houses whether the occupants wanted them there or not. At the same time Italian youth became even more highly organized; on many Saturdays my schoolmates and I had to travel to Parma to attend parades in our various uniforms. Both the Boy Scouts and the Girl Guides had been banned in Italy long since, in 1926. The Fascist youth organizations which replaced them never went camping, or learned how to cook, or developed any other outdoor skills. Except for a sports day once a year, their activities were limited to parading up and down.

I tried missing some of these parades, but one day I was summoned to the local headquarters of the organization in Parma where a rather fat, forbidding woman of high rank, dressed in Fascist uniform, told me that if I missed any more I would be suspended from school. Later on I produced a medical certificate, given me by the doctor, stating that my father was ill and that Saturdays and Sundays were the only days of the week I was at home and could help my mother look after him. This certificate produced the desired effect and I was allowed to stay at home on parade days. By some bureaucratic error I was never recalled, and because of this I never became a *Giovane Fascista*.

My father was indeed seriously ill. He had contracted acute nephritis – inflammation of the kidneys – together with high blood pressure, and his face, feet and ankles became very swollen. He was very demoralized and his recovery took many weeks. Throughout this worrying period the doctor proved a true friend; he spared no effort in helping my father regain his health, and never sent a bill.

Leeches were used to reduce the patient's blood pressure. These slimy, dark creatures were applied to his back and left there until they became so full of blood that they fell off. My mother then gathered them up and put them in a container, and I took them to a nearby stream and let them go – with goodness knows what effect on the environment. This operation was repeated until my father began to recover. It was the first time that one of us had been seriously ill.

The war in Abyssinia did not have much effect on the people of Fontanellato. Few, if any, of them had sons or relatives who took any part in it. There were no patriotic demonstrations of joy, as there were in Parma, because there were very few really ardent Fascists out in the country at that time. There were many more ardent Communists, but ever since the twenties they had been obliged to keep very quiet indeed. When in 1937 Mussolini, like Hitler, intervened in support of Franco in the Spanish Civil War, and again when he annexed Libya in October 1938, the ordinary inhabitants of Fontanellato showed an almost total lack of interest; principally, again, because none of them were involved. Whatever the Communists felt they kept to themselves.

In September 1938, when I was sixteen, I went back to my native country for a holiday; partly because I wanted to see my friends in Štanjel, and partly so that I could visit my uncles, aunts and cousins on my mother's side of the family in Mavhinje. I also wanted to see Mussolini, who was coming to Trieste on an official visit, so I wrote to my godmother's sister, Poldka, who lived there, to ask if she could put me up. I had to do this three months before Mussolini's visit because the security arrangements were intense; there were many Slavs in the city with anti-Fascist feelings. Every family had to notify the police of the number of members of the family

104

who would be present on the day, and give the names of any guests who would be staying in the house.

The local Italian paper *Il Piccolo* was full of praise for Mussolini, pointing out that Italy would have lost Trieste to the Slavs if Mussolini had not reconquered it in La Rivoluzione Fascista. Because of this, it went on, the city was bound to him for life and death and was now ready to spring to his assistance with a great display of strength. In fact Trieste, which under the Austro-Hungarian Empire had been the main port of Middle Europe, had diminished in importance as far as Italy was concerned: Genoa had effectively taken its place. On the day of Mussolini's arrival in the city *Il Piccolo* greeted him with an enigmatic front-page headline: '*Duce, Duce, Duce!* You came from the Sea!'

Before I left Fontanellato my father had told me that although he was not against my trying to see Mussolini he would be very upset if I indulged in any kind of cheering or applause. I promised I wouldn't and in fact had no intention of doing so, as I secretly regarded the Duce as a bit of a buffoon. He was known for wanting to be photographed from every conceivable angle and vigorously applauded when making his inflammatory speeches, and I was looking forward to seeing in the flesh this extraordinary man of whom my parents had brought me up to disapprove.

When the day came I got up very early and managed to get myself into what was almost the front row of the crowd, immediately underneath the platform in Piazza Unità where he was to appear. When he finally did so the impression he made was unforgettable. Wearing a rather absurd black tasselled fez, an army officer's uniform jacket, riding breeches and a black shirt, he delivered his speech slowly, articulating the words very clearly. He stood in a familiar, flamboyant posture with his hands on his hips and his chin stuck out, constantly turning his head from left to right and back again,

105

to take in his entire audience. He looked taller than I had imagined him: it was said that the platforms on which he stood always had an elevated section in the middle to raise him up. The effect he had on me was unexpected. I found his personality irresistibly magnetic and at the end of his speech I joined the rest of the huge crowd in tumultuous cheering. It was an experience I will never forget, and one of which, when I returned home, I felt deeply ashamed. I never told my parents.

Mussolini's visit passed off without incident, mainly because many people suspected of anti-Fascist sentiments had been put under arrest and because there were large numbers of security men mingling with the crowds.

I left Trieste the following morning for Mavhinje and the house of my Aunt Ema, whom I always remembered with real affection. She lived in the house where my mother had been born and had spent the first seventeen years of her life, up until the time she was married. Aunt Ema wore a scarf knotted at the back of her head in the way particular to women of the Kras, and she was always smiling. Whenever my mother and I had visited her from Štanjel, the first thing Aunt Ema always did was to call me into the larder, which was dark and cool, and give me a large spoonful of the most delicious cream from which she used to make butter, saying in the Mavhinje dialect: 'Take this, beautiful, because I know that you don't like cream in your coffee.' And then she would make coffee for my mother.

Mavhinje, like other nearby villages, had no springs of its own. The people who lived there had to rely on rainwater, which in the summer was often inadequate. Before the First World War, the younger women of the village, of whom my mother was one, used to walk from Mavhinje to Štivan (San Giovanni), near the coast, and bring back pots of water on their heads. It was a journey of several miles each way. At

Štivan, by a beautiful church, the River Timavo emerged from the Kras after a twenty-mile journey underground from the village of Skocjan in Slovenia. It was a place of idyllic beauty, and some said it was where the Argonauts had landed.

Now I was given a small, whitewashed room at the end of the long wooden balcony that ran the entire length of the house, above a courtyard shaded by long pergolas of vines. I spent a happy time in Mavhinje. With my cousin Emka, I wandered through the oak woods gathering wild flowers – the cyclamens in which the Kras is so abundant at that time of year. The wild narcissi and beautiful peonies, which liked to grow among grass or in the shade, hidden among the roots of the trees, were over. Children were now gathering vast quantities of the pale mauve cyclamens and selling them along the main road to Trieste or at the railway station at Sesljan (Sistiana). Some, older and more ambitious, took large baskets full of flowers all the way to Trieste, about fourteen miles away by train, and sold them there.

At this time of my life I was eagerly reading books of travel and adventure such as Luigi Barzini's *Peking to Paris by Motor Car*, but my favourite writer was Salgari, who was a sort of Italian Jules Verne. Books of adventure, of which Dr Sambataro was a generous lender, convinced me that nothing exciting would ever happen in Fontanellato. But I was still far too young to venture out in the world; it was unheard of even for an older girl to leave her home and family and become independent. Girls, even upper-class girls, stayed at home until they were married; and if they never married they stayed at home for good. What I had to look forward to at best, so far as I could see, was marriage with a worthy young man such as Paolo, with whom I already felt myself to be in love, then children and a life of boring respectability in the Pianura Padana.

Shortly after my visit to Mavhinje, and completely unexpectedly, the news was brought to me of Paolo's death from meningitis in the hospital in Parma.

I was shattered by this news. It was as if a great void had opened and I could not at first believe that there would be no more visits to the *balere* with him. It was fortunate that I had a good friend of my own age, also called Wanda: we relished being gloomy together. We talked for hours on end about the existence or otherwise of God, the futility of human life, and all the other things that sixteen-year-old girls find to discuss.

One afternoon we became so depressed that we decided to drown our sorrows in drink. Wanda stole a half-bottle of Latvian double kümmel from her father's extensive cellar and we took it to a little bridge on the outskirts of the village where we sat and talked, being careful to hide the bottle when anyone passed by but sipping away until we had finished the lot. We were not used to drinking anything more than a glass of watered wine with our meals, and the effect on us, while not immediate, was catastrophic. I only just managed to get back to our house before collapsing into bed. Fortunately my mother was out. The other Wanda was equally ill, and equally lucky: her mother too was out when she got home. I was sick all night and felt terrible for two days, so terrible that my mother called in Dr Sambataro. I don't know what his diagnosis was but I don't think either of them even vaguely suspected alcohol.

I was lucky to be able to go to school in Parma and not spend all my life in Fontanellato, which was the fate of many; and on the whole my schooldays were enjoyable. It was good to be in a class with so few girls; there were just three of us among fourteen boys, and as a result we all became good friends without forming any sentimental attachments. We helped each other with homework and went together to the Giardino Pubblico when we finished lessons early.

I always enjoyed listening to the Parmigiani in the class. They had a very good sense of humour and could tell long, sophisticated stories in what is called the *spaccato*, the real dialect of Parma. We seldom discussed politics but I knew that even though they belonged officially to a Fascist organization their sentiments were more inclined to the local brand of Communism.

In Parma, as in all other towns and cities in Italy, there were a number of *case di tolleranza*, brothels recognized by the authorities, in which the girls were subject to regular medical examinations, and three of the boys in our class plucked up the courage to visit one of these on the way home from school one evening.

The next morning, during break, I noticed that they were all unusually quiet, and could not understand why. Finally they told me where they had been and how they had been ushered into a sort of waiting room by the proprietress, who had endeavoured to make them feel at ease by offering them *marrons glacés*. Girls of various shapes and sizes paraded in front of the boys while she told them the prices so that they would be sure they had enough money on them. When it came to choosing a girl they were all much too shy and simply took what they were offered. Although by now they were rather subdued, they had apparently acquitted themselves quite satisfactorily, and all three said, without going into details, that it had been a wonderful, albeit expensive, experience. I was very impressed.

In September 1939, when war broke out in the West, almost everyone in our part of the world believed that Mussolini would join in as an ally of Hitler; in 1936 the German alliance with Italy, the Berlin-Rome Axis, had been established. In the event Mussolini remained neutral. Italy's involvement in the Spanish Civil War, in emulation of Germany, had cost much more than the government had intended, and by 1939 Mussolini must have known that the Army and Air Force were not anything like as strong as he had imagined they were, even if he did not know the extent of their weakness. What was then a rumour – that the same units were moved from one place to another for his inspections – proved to be the truth.

For us in Italy, war finally came on 10 June 1940, when Mussolini declared war on France, which was already on its knees, and on Britain, whose soldiers had been driven out of Europe. It was a warm, sunny June day in Fontanellato and I was riding out into the country on my bicycle when another cyclist gave me the news.

I remember experiencing a feeling of tremendous excitement, not thinking for a moment of the implications of war, of bombing, of deaths, of families parted from their sons, husbands and brothers. I just thought that the war would be fought far away, like the one in Abyssinia, and that it would be over in a few days, or weeks at the most.

When I went home my excitement soon evaporated. I found my mother very distressed. She knew what war was about, having lived through one already. In the First World War her village, Mavhinje, had been under fire in the Austro-Hungarian front line at the foot of the Hermada. On the forward slopes of this mountain, towards Monfalcone, terrible and bloody battles had been fought. With my father away at the war, she had been forced to leave her home and became a refugee in a village in Slovenia near Ljubljana. Now, for a second great war, she found herself in a country which was not her own; although she had made a few friends, it was not at all like living among her own people. She never, as she had done in Štanjel, went to visit families on sudden impulse. If anything she had become even more religious than before, and seemed to find serenity and peace in going to church at least three times a week. She also found great pleasure in reading, but although my father had brought to Fontanellato a large number of Slovene books, she had soon to resort to reading in Italian, which she inevitably found more difficult. She accepted the news of war with bewilderment and sadness; feelings she soon learned to keep to herself. During all the long years of the war it was she who kept up the morale of all of us, especially my father, who went through many difficult times.

In the days which followed the declaration of war, the press did its best to inspire enthusiasm in the Italian people and build confidence in the belief that victory was inevitable; backed by this propaganda, Mussolini ordered the invasion of Greece in October of the same year. By December the invading forces were being held by the defenders, but the press, heavily scrutinized by Mussolini, kept a very low profile about it. As battles were lost, Italian journalists stressed that success would come as a result of Italian cleverness, led by the Duce, and because the Italians were so imaginative and cultured and brave.

During the first months of war life in Fontanellato was uneventful and the fighting seemed far away. I continued to go to school in Parma and life there seemed very uneventful too. We read in the papers of continuous victories on all fronts, which gave us the impression that the war would be over soon. The advances in Abyssinia and Somalia did not raise any excitement in our village. There were not many foods in short supply – only sugar, which we missed more than anything else. The only Fontanellato events recorded in the local paper were the bicycle race, the 25-kilometre race, and the bowling competition, of which my father was a great supporter.

In that summer of 1940 the first few families began to leave town and come to live in their country *ville* outside Fontanellato. One of the first was the Camattini family, who left La Spezia, the great port and naval base on the Ligurian Sea which everyone expected to be bombarded by the British Fleet. They had a high-class shop there selling dress materials and men's suiting, and they brought the most valuable stock with them to store in their villa. The Camattini had two daughters of approximately my age with whom I soon became good friends, Maria Vittoria and Renata. They had left school that summer, not wishing to study any more, and Fontanellato was to be their home until the end of the war. To meet new people meant a lot to me because those of my Fontanellato friends who had not gone to school in Parma had already started work. Ada was helping her father, the local postman, and had to run the house for her old mother; Nives had opened a hairdresser's shop; and Nora was already apprenticed to a tailor.

I had enough girlfriends in Fontanellato never to be bored, but I only had very little money to spend. School, books, tram fares to Parma and clothing were all my parents could manage, because a schoolmaster's salary was very low. In 1940 I was fortunate to find a summer job in the local tomato factory, one of the innumerable similar factories scattered in the Parma province. This one gathered all the tomatoes from the surrounding country and made *salsa di pomodoro*, tomato sauce, which was sold in tins. I was in charge of weekly wages and organized shifts and hours, as well as keeping a check on the quantities of tomatoes brought in and weighed at the entrance of the factory. At the height of the season, July and August, the quantities were enormous, and the carts or trucks had to queue outside on the road. There was a constant stream of them from early morning all through the day, but my work ended at five in the afternoon, when I was free to go and meet my friends.

The owners of the factory were three partners. One of them was an architect who, even at the age of sixty, was very handsome and likeable, and I fell in love with him. I don't know if he ever guessed my feelings but he always treated me with great kindness and understanding. He used to visit the factory rather late in the afternoon and, if I knew he was coming, I would wait there for him under some pretext. The rush was over by then, so I had time to listen to him telling me how bored he had been with the monotonous life in Parma. Years before, he had temporarily escaped, and gone to work in Panama when the building of the Canal was in progress between 1904 and 1914. I was spellbound: I had never known anybody who had been to such a faraway country. But when my summer job ended my infatuation ended with it.

In October 1940 my last year at school began; it was going to be a year of hard work, as I had to prepare for the June examinations. I wanted a diploma because I knew that there was no possibility of my going to a university. I would have liked to have gone to Venice, where there was a faculty of languages, or Bologna, where I could have read Economics and Commerce; but the war was on, and the expense of keeping me in a distant town was beyond the means of my parents.

In September and October we read in the papers of the heavy raids on London, and the more we read and heard about them the more difficult it became to understand how people could survive. We could not conceive of such things happening to us.

At around this time I began to give private lessons in Latin and mathematics to a few boys who were in their first and second years of school in Parma or who had to take an entrance examination. I found it very hard work. I would arrive home late in the afternoon, and by the time I had had something to eat and done some of my own homework the first pupil had arrived. The children, I thought, were not particularly bright and they found any sort of work very difficult. I had to repeat things again and again, hoping that something would sink in, but I was rewarded for my efforts with the satisfaction of knowing that they all passed their examinations at the end of the year. I was paid for the lessons not in money but in food, so we always had enough oil, sugar, cheese and butter – commodities that were now difficult to obtain. One of my pupils was the son of a grocer, and the parents of another owned *caseifici*, small Parmigiano cheese factories. I continued to give lessons all through the war, as food got scarcer and scarcer.

Life in Parma at the beginning of the school year seemed normal apart from the Fascist propaganda in the papers, but one began to sense that the members of the Party were becoming even more arrogant and domineering than before, and that it was increasingly important for people with different ideas to keep them to themselves and never to discuss politics. One did not see uniformed members of the Partito Nazionale Fascista walking about the streets every day, but from time to time there were parades in which they could easily be identified. By December 1940 the news from the African front was very bad so far as Italy was concerned. The British had launched a powerful attack, and first Mersa Matruh (which Mussolini had planned to enter in triumph) fell, then Bardia and Tobruk. This was a catastrophic defeat, and altogether 113,000 Italian prisoners were captured. By the following February Italy had lost Somalia. The British captured Eritrea, and on 5 May the Emperor of Abyssinia returned to Addis Ababa, five years after leaving it. 'The Libyan desert has become an inferno where the front line moves continuously as if it had gone mad,' wrote Monelli, an Italian war correspondent. The Ministry of Propaganda did what it could to play down such disasters and tried for as long as possible to preserve the illusion that they were not important, but Fascism now began to lose a lot of its popular support.

One day in the spring of 1941, as I was walking with my schoolfriend Wilma in Via Cavour, the elegant street in the centre of Parma, we saw two men go up to another who was quietly reading the paper outside a café. They stood him on his feet and punched him mercilessly until he fell to the ground. Nobody intervened, although there were many people walking in the street, and when the two men had finished what they had obviously planned to do, they left as unhurriedly as they had come. Wilma and I were horrified and frightened: we had never seen such a scene before. Then we heard somebody who was nearby murmur in a low voice, 'They were Fascists.'

I could not believe that such an outburst of violence could happen in Fontanellato, where everybody, including those who belonged to the Party, seemed to be more or less on good terms with one another, but when I arrived home I begged my father to be careful and to avoid discussions with anybody except the doctor.

In the spring we were all working hard to prepare for the June exams, when we were told that for that year, because of the war, examinations would be abolished. A committee of professors, who were also our teachers, would judge us on the marks we had had during the past four years, especially this last year, and award diplomas accordingly. I was greatly relieved, both because this decision was going to save me endless work in revision and because I knew that if all my marks over the year were taken into account I should not have any problem in passing.

115

In June 1941, *Anno XIX Era Fascista*, I became a *ragioniera*, an accountant; the diploma I received entitled me to put the *Rag.* in front of my name. In the same month Germany invaded Russia. In Verona Mussolini reviewed the first Italian troops to go to Russia: the Julia division of the Alpini.

Dr Sambataro felt very strongly about the decision to send troops to Russia; he had a lot to do with the army in the course of his work. 'How', he asked, 'can Mussolini send the boys to fight in a country where the winters are so incredibly cold and for which the Italian Army, even the Alpini, are so badly equipped? Many of them do not have proper boots, or even socks. They will die of cold. It is murder.' As he foretold, thousands of Alpini lost their lives and never returned. One of them was my friend Ada's brother, a men's hairdresser. He desperately tried to pull strings with people he knew in Parma so that he would not be called up, but eventually he had to go. He wrote home often, trying to keep his family's spirits up, but between the lines one could read that life was not good. Eventually he stopped writing and was never heard of again. The family had great hopes, after the war, that he would suddenly reappear (some soldiers did eventually return, years later), and kept all his hairdressing equipment clean and unused and all his clothes under dust sheets well into the 1970s. He probably lies somewhere out on the Steppes, together with so many of his companions.

As soon as I left school I found work in the local Banca Nazionale dell'Agricoltura. Before being taken on I was asked to go to Parma because the 'Big Boss', as he was called, wanted to interview me. I found it gratifying to be offered a job without searching for one. I went to meet him and was deeply disappointed to discover that the head of a bank could be such a short, bald, rather fat individual. As I talked to him, however, I soon realized that he had a great aura of authority and self-assurance. We talked about the implications of the job and agreed on a salary, and I became a member of the bank.

Although during the years I worked there I had the opportunity to meet many people, mainly the farmers who were our principal customers, I can honestly say that my job was the most boring and monotonous I could possibly have had. I worked directly under the Manager, Signor Cavatorta, who was very able and extremely diplomatic with his customers, and I learnt how indifferent and merciless all banks are towards any customer who has the misfortune to be in debt: that was more or less all.

It was during the summer of 1941 that I met Valeria Cantoni, a girl whose parents owned land and a fine farmhouse at Ghiaie, near Fontanellato. I had not seen her before because during the school year she lived in Parma, where the family had a house, and during the holidays she was taken either to the sea or to the mountains. She was dark and beautiful, and when she laughed with her eyes shut and showed her white teeth, her skin looked even darker. Born of a Jewish mother and a Catholic father, she was the most wonderful storyteller. Her stories lasted for hours and were full of detail and humour . . .

Her father was always very elegant, never without his hat, a Borsalino, and often smoking a thin cigar. He always spoke in the Parma dialect and was hardly ever at home except for meals or to see the farmers. He was wealthy, but it was rumoured that he was a heavy gambler and lost large sums in Monte Carlo. As a young man he had had a strong desire to visit the United States and decided to go there for a holiday, but as the liner approached New York, he dreamed that his mother (to whom he was not particularly strongly attached) was lonely and missed him, and this dream made him terribly homesick. Having hardly set foot on American soil, and without a second thought, he boarded the next liner and sailed back. From the day he returned his friends called him 'Cantoni l'Americano', and this nickname remained with him until he died.

When people, especially women, are in need of help or comfort, they turn to the Virgin of Fontanellato and pray, in the hope that their prayers will be answered. After her marriage Signor Cantoni's mother had seemed unable to bear a child so she took a large bunch of carnations to the Madonna and asked her for the gift of a baby. Her prayers were eventually answered, but after the birth of her first longed-for child she had four more. It was more than she had bargained for, and she now returned to the Madonna with a much bigger bunch of flowers praying fervently for an end to her fertility.

As an old woman, many years later, she asked her son to take her to the sea, which she had heard of but never seen. He took her in his car up to one of the few routes over the Apennines, but when she arrived at the pass, the Passo della Cisa, and saw the undulating, never-ending hills, she panicked. '*Com'é grande il mondo*,' she said. 'How big the world is. I don't want to go any further; please take me back home!'

These were three of Valeria's stories. They were always flavoured with her subtle Parmigiano-Jewish humour and could captivate any audience. She didn't talk much about her mother, who was rather withdrawn and authoritarian and spent most of her time playing bridge or playing the piano.

During 1942 other evacuee families started to arrive in Fontanellato, some from Milan and some from other cities, feeling that life in the country was safer. If they did not own property, they rented rooms wherever they could find them. Holidays at the seaside or in the mountains were by now out of the question, but for young people it was still a wonderful summer: the war seemed far away, and there was enough to eat even if it was rationed. We read in the papers about the German war in Russia but we only knew one boy who was fighting there: Ada's brother. We all met every evening and sat under the trees discussing films we had seen, books we were reading and radio programmes we had heard. As soon as I started work part of my salary went towards buying a radio. I bought it in instalments from a man in the village; it was a wonderful Art Deco radio which proved indestructible.

Our bicycles were in constant use. We laughed and flirted and often went to swim in the Torrente Taro. There was very little water flowing, but the rains and the melted snow in the spring left large pools which were reasonably clear and clean since nobody swam in them but us. At weekends we cycled there under the hot sun in the early afternoon, not minding the heat at all because we knew that as soon as we arrived the cool water would welcome us. We were told by our parents that it was bad for our health to drink a lot of water in such heat, so we all became very thin, as well as very brown, in the sun.

If we didn't go to swim, Valeria's house was always open to us. Most of the time her mother was not there; or if she was she didn't appear. We played cards, listened to records and danced. Valeria had a wind-up gramophone and many records, among them some American ones like 'Smoke Gets in Your Eyes', 'Begin the Beguine', 'Waltz Triste' adapted for dancing, and many others. We also had wonderful refreshments; my favourites were shortcrust pastry boats filled with delicious fresh cream. There was always a choice of tea with lemon, cool sweet *moscato* white wine or *malvasia* from Torrechiara, a village in the hills.

All this soon came to an abrupt end. Valeria had asked us for the afternoon and suggested that we should stay on for the evening, as her mother had gone to spend the night with a friend. I asked my parents if they would allow me to stay the night, saying that Valeria was alone in the house and I would keep her company. In fact there were about ten of us, five girls and five boys, including one handsome boy with whom Valeria was in love. The afternoon went like lightning, and we ate a very delicious cold supper. More games followed, including a quiz in which anyone who gave a wrong answer had to remove an item of clothing: before long we were all left in nothing but our underpants. At this stage we decided to end the game and start dancing. We danced until the early hours of the morning when, exhausted, we all went together to a large bedroom and fell asleep. Late in the morning Valeria suggested we should all go down and have breakfast, and as we came down the staircase we saw to our horror that her mother was waiting for us at the bottom. It was as if hammers had hit us; without a word we left, and we did not set foot in the house for many months, until Valeria announced that all was forgiven.

Looking back I find it hard to believe that I didn't keep abreast of all the war news; but the war had been going on for so long that I, like almost every girl of my generation, had lost interest in it. Propaganda had given us indigestion, and reports of how many aeroplanes had been destroyed and how many ships had been sunk were becoming monotonous if not unbelievable. Were the Allies so bad at war that they were incapable of any victories?

We had continuous news from the front, but unless it involved someone we knew, it had little effect on us. All the ordinary Italian wanted was an end to the war, but it was difficult to imagine a world ruled by Nazis, Fascists and the Japanese. What did we know about Japan? *Madame Butterfly* at the Teatro Regio in Parma did not offer us much in the way of solid information.

By the end of 1942, the great year of success for the Axis, things were starting to change dramatically. Rommel was in full retreat in Africa and the Allies re-entered Tobruk. The press played down these reverses, and they paled into insignificance when in spring 1943 word spread that a prisoner-of-war camp was going to be set up on the outskirts of Fontanellato. For the village it was the most exciting news in living memory. Nobody knew for certain which building was going to be used, but there was a strong rumour that it was going to be the *orfanotrofio*, the orphanage. This was a large mock-classical brick building, with columns and pediments. It had been begun in 1928 by Padre Mazzetti, of the Dominican fathers in the Santuario, but had never been finished or occupied up until now. According to one or two bold spirits who had succeeded in getting into it, it was so badly constructed that when they jumped up and down on the floor the entire building trembled.

One day, towards the end of March, the whole place became a hive of activity. Soldiers set up barbed-wire fences, electricians wired up searchlights, carpenters built barracks and sentry boxes on elevated platforms.

By 30 March the building was ready but empty. The following morning 650 English-speaking officers and soldiers from all over the Empire arrived. Apparently they had come by train the previous night to the nearby station of Fidenza, from various camps in southern Italy. In the course of the journey one of them, an RAF pilot, had been shot dead trying to jump out of the train in an attempt to reach an Italian fighter plane on an airfield and fly it to Yugoslavia.

Everyone, young and old, was very impatient to see the prisoners; most of us, including me, had never seen an Englishman before. We couldn't often see them from the main road which passed in front of the building because they were forbidden to look out of the windows. If they did look out the sentries had orders to fire on them, which they did from time to time although no one was ever injured. The only reliable

121

way to see them was to pass in front of the building and turn left into the road to the cemetery: from that side some of them could be seen craning out of the windows and waving.

It is the custom all over Italy to visit the cemetery and take flowers to the graves, usually on Sundays or on the anniversary of a death. Once the prisoners had arrived, the dead found themselves in perpetual company. Never could they have been visited by so many young girls.

At first the prisoners had only a very small piece of wired-in exercise ground at the back of the orphanage, but later, on humanitarian grounds, the Italian Colonel was forced to relent and extend it by wiring in an extra expanse of rough ground about a hundred metres square. The prisoners, under strict supervision, were allowed to level it so that they could play football or a strange game called rugby, or go running, or simply sit in the sun.

From the heavily wired enclosure, in which the prisoners were allowed from 10 a.m. until 5 p.m., two daring escapes were made. Under cover of the rugby-players, who surrounded them so that they were invisible to the sentries, two officers managed to bury themselves underground, where they remained until darkness: they then came to the surface and made their escape. They succeeded in stealing a fishing boat and crossing the Po, and were only recaptured near Lake Como, where they were about to cross the frontier into Switzerland. They had been free for nearly a month.

Three days later, three more officers did the same thing. Two of them, disguised as Spanish workers, walked the seventeen kilometres to Parma where they caught a train to Milan, and were arrested on the way. The third, who had become separated from them, lost his shirt, and was so dirty that he was arrested at Parma station.

Twice a week, having given their word of honour that they would not attempt to escape, those prisoners who wished to go for a heavily guarded march through the surrounding countryside, along lanes chosen for their loneliness, were allowed to do so. They were never allowed into Fontanellato or any of the surrounding villages, and people were forbidden to wave to them. They marched at a tremendous rate in all sorts of uniforms – one of them had amazing cherry-red trousers – and all their clothing was marked with big red patches. Some of them were very tall, some were very blond, some had big moustaches. They laughed and joked all the time, and deliberately exhausted their guards by making them walk too fast.

Suddenly, on 10 July, the Allies invaded Sicily, and on 26 July we heard on the radio the astonishing news that Mussolini had been deposed and arrested and that the King had invited General Badoglio to form a new government. The Duce had been reduced in a stroke from Head of State to a more or less insignificant *cavaliere* (a commonplace title in Italy). People were delirious with joy. They smashed pictures of the Duce, tore down posters and obliterated the boastful slogans painted on the sides of houses.

The only people who suffered were the prisoners, who were not allowed to go for walks any more.

IV

Armistice

IT WAS Wednesday 8 September 1943, the second great *festa* of the year for the Madonna of Fontanellato. The last pilgrims had gone home, and the small kiosks and stalls were closing. My girlfriends and I were out making the *passeggiata*. Although it had been a very warm day, the evening had a slight feeling of autumn: it was particularly beautiful, with the sun turning the leaves of the trees a marvellous golden colour. All of us were wearing something new – a *spianato* – because it was the custom, however difficult in years of war, to have a new outfit for this occasion which marked the beginning of autumn.

We were strolling along, laughing and joking, when Amelio, a kind of village clown who never seemed to take anything seriously (and who was never taken seriously himself), approached us on his bicycle in a state of great excitement. 'Have you heard the news? Badoglio has asked the Allies for an armistice; the war is over. I just heard it on the radio.' And he disappeared to find other people to tell.

At first we did not believe him. We knew that the radio news was not transmitted at that time of day, so we decided it was just another of his silly jokes. But as we walked we began to notice mounting excitement among the people in the streets and in the cafés. The news had spread like wildfire.

I rushed home, where my mother was alone, but she knew already. We stayed close to the radio and eventually heard a repeat of what proved to be Marshal Badoglio's first and last broadcast to the nation, uttered in a mournful voice:

'The Italian Government, recognizing the impossibility of continuing the unequal struggle against the overwhelming enemy power, with the intent of saving further and more serious disasters to the Nation, has asked an armistice of General Eisenhower, Commander-in-Chief of the Anglo-American forces. The request has been granted.'

That night a curfew was announced to start at 11 p.m. and Parma was occupied by the SS Panzer Division Adolf Hitler.

The next day no one talked of anything but the armistice, speculating on what was going to happen. Would the Germans withdraw or stand and fight? Would there be bloodshed if and when they pulled out? We were surrounded by Germans: they were in every town and in the country too.

Soon rumours started that the prisoners in the orphanage would be set free but no one knew where they would go. Some people talked of Switzerland. At a quarter to one on 9 September the Commandant of the camp, Colonello Vicedomini, ordered the doors to be opened and the barbed wire cut. As soon as these orders had been carried out the prisoners started to leave. A large number of villagers, including my father and me, went to watch the exodus of the prisoners, which was led by the senior British Colonel. In their hundreds they set out calmly from the back of the building, through the exercise field towards the open country. Some were laughing, some talking, some silent. Among them was a young officer who was riding a mule (which stubbornly stopped from time to time) and roaring with laughter. I had seen him once before when he had waved to me from an upper window and I had waved back. Later I learned that he had injured his ankle running up and down stairs in the building in order to keep fit; the leg was very painful and he could not walk. None of us could imagine where the mule came from.

After the prisoners had left, some boys, feeling rather brave, entered the building to see if there was anything left in it. No one seemed to be in charge of it. They brought out large packs of cigarettes – then rationed – and shared them out among the men who were on the road watching.

My father could not believe his luck. For him, a heavy smoker, this was manna sent from heaven: he now had a large supply to keep him going. The boys were about to go into the building again after their first successful looting when suddenly somebody shouted: '*I Tedeschi, i Tedeschi arrivano!*' 'The Germans, the Germans are coming!' And there on the road we saw a number of German lorries approaching, loaded with soldiers wearing steel helmets. Everything was so sudden that we didn't know what to do, whether to stay where we were or to run. After all, why should they hurt us? We were nothing to do with the prison camp or the escaped prisoners. So we stayed where we were and waited with apprehension to see what would happen.

Suddenly there was a lot of firing and the camp guards fled. With my father, who was trying to protect me and his cigarettes at the same time, I jumped into a nearby ditch which ran parallel to the road. In fact the Germans were firing into the air, although we did not realize it at the time, so there were no casualties. The camp was empty apart from the Italian Colonel, who bravely assumed full responsibility for letting the prisoners go.

The Germans did not even bother to look for the escaped prisoners. Instead they placed the Colonello under arrest and took him away. Later he was sent to a concentration camp in Germany, where he underwent a lot of suffering and privation, and died on his return to Italy after the war was over. He was too honourable: he should have disappeared with the rest of his men.

The Germans left with their prey, and no one knew if they

were going to return, but all through the night and for several days more the orphanage was looted. Blankets, vests, pants, shirts, socks, shoes, tins of food, tea, cigarettes – everything was taken. Rumour had it that two young men had even tried to remove a large piano. They were successful in taking it as far as the stairs, but when they tried to bring it down it slipped, nearly killing one of them.

Some bold people had contrived to take away so much stuff that later, when clothing became very short, they were able to conduct a very lucrative business on the black market. No one had much success with the tinned food, though, whether it was bully beef or the unnaturally sweet Spam. No one in the Po valley, with its rich agriculture, could bring themselves to eat such concoctions. Even more mysterious were the tins of pre-mixed tea, milk and sugar, to which people tried to add water. Most of the food was wasted.

Now that the Colonello had been taken away, the only Italian from the camp who remained was one of the two interpreters, Capitano Camino, who had an excellent command of English because he had been a businessman in England before the war. While I had liked the Colonello very much, because of his courteous way of talking to me, I never really took to Camino – who seemed more English than the English with his stiff upper lip – although subsequently he behaved very well.

Before the camp was liberated the senior British colonel in command of it had already chosen a temporary hiding place for the prisoners. It was not a very good one, but there was little choice in such a dead-flat plain. It was to the north-west of the village about one and a half kilometres away, on the banks of a stream called the Rovacchia, behind a grass embankment. There, and among the rows of vines, the escapers remained hidden, not knowing what to do next or where to go.

130

It was fortunate that the weather was good and they could sleep in the open, but that did not solve the immediate problem of how they were to be fed. Camino came to see me in the bank and asked if the village girls would be prepared to collect food and take it on their bicycles to the prisoners. He said that we should travel in pairs – never more than two at a time – so as not to arouse suspicion if we met any Germans or Fascists.

The situation was chaotic. No one seemed to know who was in charge of the country. None of us realized that Badoglio, who had ordered the armed forces to resist the Germans, had already fled Italy, together with the King, and left it leaderless.

My family was not in a position to give much food, so I went to Valeria to ask if she could help. We asked her mother who, in spite of being Jewish and already in a precarious position, did not hesitate for a moment. She prepared baskets full of food; not only bread and cheese and wine, but also roast chickens, cooked rabbits, salami and any other supplies she could lay her hands on. Her farm was a rich one and there was no shortage of produce. Every day she prepared fresh food for us to take. My mother and our neighbours helped with everything they could. We also managed to get tins of the famous, unappreciated Spam and bully beef back from the looters and, knowing that the English liked strong tea, we boiled up more of their mixture for them, producing something of an indescribable colour that was more like a meal than a drink.

It was not difficult to find the place where the prisoners were hiding. When we reached it I called out in my broken English: 'Where are you? We have come to bring you food. Do not be afraid.'

We waited. There was silence. We called again and then saw, creeping under the vines with a finger over his mouth

131

to urge silence, a tall, blond young man who uttered the only word of Italian he knew: '*Grazie.*' We followed him to where two of his companions were hiding under a row of vines. All three were still dressed in what they had been wearing in the camp: corduroy trousers, khaki shirts and pullovers and big nailed boots. We introduced ourselves and told them we had brought them some food which they could share with their friends. They laughed when they saw the tea, and demonstrated in dumb show how it should really be made.

We tried to tell them that they were in as safe a place as possible, that only reliable people knew where they were hiding, and that we would come again the next day. We also promised to try to gather together some civilian clothes for them and their companions; as they were, they looked much too English and conspicuous. Their names were Donald, Ian and Hugo, and they told us that they were extremely grateful for all the food but that the last thing they wanted was to put us in any danger: they begged us not to come again because there would almost certainly be someone in the village who would denounce us to the Germans or the Fascists.

We did not promise; but before we went back I asked them what had happened to the prisoner who had looked so funny escaping on a mule. They said he had been taken to a nearby farmhouse where he was being given shelter for the time being, and that his name was Eric. All this conversation was carried on with the greatest difficulty. Ian was the best at making himself understood as he had been a Latin scholar. Relieved of the weight of the food in our panniers we returned to Fontanellato, where the latest news was not too good.

The Germans, already in the country in large numbers, had seized Rome, and Hitler had ordered the setting up of a political system which would take effective control of the country and also take under its wing any future Fascist administration. What concerned us more was the news that

132

anyone sheltering or helping escaped prisoners-of-war would be severely punished. For the Germans, the thought that the thousands of prisoners-of-war now free behind their lines might take up arms was a continuing nightmare.

That evening Valeria and I discussed the problem of whether to carry on with our mission or not. We soon came to the same decision, which was that having promised the boys we would help them, we couldn't now let them down. After all, we thought (quite irrationally and knowing next to nothing about the Germans), even if they met two young girls cycling in the countryside, they would never suspect us of taking food and clothing to the English.

The next day we went again to the Rovacchia but this time I insisted we should also go and see the crazy Englishman who had ridden the mule. I knew the farmer who was hiding him, Signor Merli, because I had often met him in the bank, and I knew he was a very honest and reliable man who would never betray anybody.

When we got to the farm, which was in a hamlet called Paroletta, the doctor was already there. He and Capitano Camino were discussing the future of the prisoner, who was still unable to walk because of his painful damaged ankle. The only option, as far as the doctor was concerned, was to get him into the local hospital where he would be well looked after and out of sight for the time being. I had already heard about this plan because the doctor had discussed it with my father; but it was apparent that Eric himself was not at all enthusiastic about it.

'Eric,' I said in my just-understandable English. 'We are only trying to help you. If the doctor says you must go to hospital, then you must go. With your foot in that condition you cannot go very far. It is only for the time being. I will come and see you and teach you Italian and you will help me with my English.'

Even dressed as he now was, in a blue cotton jacket and trousers, he could never have been taken for an Italian, and since he wasn't able to walk – he could only hop on one leg – or speak the language, he was hardly likely to remain free for long out in the open. I was happy that he was being made to go to the hospital to have his ankle set in plaster, and because I found him very *simpatico* I was determined to go and see him there.

On 11 September the German *Standortkommandantur*, which had been set up in the Piazza Garibaldi to administer the city of Parma, issued a series of orders, one of which stated that it was forbidden for civilians to have guns and that looting would be punishable by death. By this time the looting of the orphanage had ceased because everything removable had already been removed.

The next day we returned to the Rovacchia with more food for the boys, but as we started walking towards the embankment we heard a woman shouting at us: 'Where is Anna? You crazy girls, go and hide. The Germans are in the village. They will surely come and arrest you. Oh, where is Anna? Where is my daughter?'

She was nearly hysterical, with some reason if what she said about the Germans was true, but we had not seen Anna. We knew her and we also knew that she was taking food to a different set of prisoners; they were beginning to scatter over an increasingly wide area as there was now no hope of an immediate Allied invasion of northern Italy, which was what everyone had hoped for. When Anna's mother finally got home she would find her daughter waiting for her, having safely accomplished her mission.

But now Valeria and I were in a quandary. If we returned to the road with our panniers full of food and met the Germans, they would probably stop and search us. We decided that the best thing to do was to hide the bicycles and the panniers separately – which was sensible – and then take refuge with the prisoners beyond the embankment until the storm was over – which was not. We didn't tell them about the Germans because we didn't want them to be more worried than they were already. Instead we made them talk about where they lived and about their families. We laughed a lot, made fun of them and their new outfits, and then, when nothing happened, we went home. On the way three big German transport planes flew overhead, scattering thousands of leaflets printed in Italian which stated that Badoglio had deserted his country – as if we didn't know this already.

When we got back to the village we found a lot of Germans milling around. They were tough-looking *Feldgendarmen*, military policemen, with big brass plaques on their chests. Armed with machine guns, they were members of a unit we soon learned to fear. They had been brought here to round up the escaped prisoners but fortunately no one was giving them any information. I found my father talking to some of them; he had been called on to act as an interpreter. I shall never forget his expression when he saw me arriving on my bicycle with its empty pannier bags. After a while the *Feldgendarmen* left without searching the surrounding countryside. Fortunately, like the majority of the members of the *carabinieri* at that time, they were not notable for their intelligence.

The next day Signor Merli came to the bank, ostensibly on business, and whispered to me that some of the prisoners had decided to leave their hiding places and strike out across the Via Emilia towards the high Apennines. The doctor had left instructions as to where they were to go and how they were to get there. Up in the remote villages they would be reasonably safe and the people would help them. A few remained among the vines, and to them we continued to take food.

After work that day, 13 September, I went to the hospital and asked to see Suor Eusebia, the Mother Superior, a truly saintly woman. In spite of the obvious dangers involved she had no objection to my trying to teach Eric Italian.

'Poor boy,' she said. 'He needs all the help we can give him and he must learn to speak Italian. He won't get far with those infinitive verbs he uses at the moment. You can teach him, but I cannot allow you to go and see him dressed as you are. You go home and change and come back.'

I knew what she meant. I had tried to make myself look pretty good. I blushed, got on my bicycle, went home and returned more suitably clad. When Suor Eusebia saw me she greeted me with an approving smile.

The hospital was a building on two floors with a large shady tree outside. It had a canopy over the entrance on which was inscribed in large letters 'Ospedale Civile Peracchi'; Peracchi being the name of its benefactor. At the back was a large and flourishing vegetable garden, the pride of the hospital gardener. The reason the vegetables were so luscious was that they were abundantly nourished with the contents of the *pozzo nero*, the hospital cesspit.

On warm days those of the hospital's old people who were still mobile used to sit and chatter under the tree in front of the building, watching the passers-by. With them was always Maria, a mongol girl who was about nine but looked older because of her stout figure, short, thick neck and large head. She was a very affectionate child and every time I went to visit Eric she held me very tight – she was extraordinarily strong – and kissed me. She always smiled and only put on an angry face when she was being teased.

Eric was in a room that formed part of the maternity ward – unless a woman in labour was brought in, it was private and quiet: the only place in the hospital that was. (A fine baby boy was born the day Eric arrived, and asked what he thought the child should be called he suggested 'Armistizio'.)

Every afternoon, after leaving the bank, I went to the

136

A group of schoolfriends in Fontanellato, 1935

Valeria *(right)* and I

With my friends Wilma and the other Wanda *(left and right)*

My friends and I cycling in Fontanellato, 1940

Valeria on the Lido in Venice

Graduation day photograph: June 1941

Santa Croce, Florence, April 1946

hospital to teach him Italian. At the beginning I found it hard work because he did not seem able to concentrate. Rather than stay in a stuffy room we decided to carry on with our lessons out of sight of the road in the back garden, which was more distracting but more pleasant.

I knew, of course, that one or other of the *suore* kept a constant eye on how we behaved, and I knew too that had they noticed anything 'unusual' I would have been given a severe talking-to and told not to come back. I had to be rather strict with my teaching. I insisted that Eric should take it seriously and, as he had nothing else to do, work hard at his grammar, because I knew that if he left the hospital knowing hardly any Italian he would surely be recaptured. It was the conjugation of verbs that he found most difficult; he expressed everything in infinitives. There were two signs which gave prisoners away: their primitive Italian and the way they walked, lifting their heels and walking briskly, as if they were flying.

But Eric found it difficult to work. He was free, he was well fed and looked after, and he had a girl who came to see him every day. 'If you don't work hard and learn the verbs, I will not come any more. You will have to find another teacher,' I told him. I made him repeat and repeat the lessons until they started to sink in and became easier. After a bit we both found the grammar rather monotonous and tried a little conversation so that my English would benefit too. Soon, as Eric's ears became accustomed to the Italian language, we were able to talk about ourselves, our dreams, our aspirations and our families. Although we didn't realize it, the books we used were becoming a tie between us, and the hours we spent together were becoming more and more enjoyable. In fact we were slowly falling in love, and when one late afternoon Eric kissed me as we were leaving the garden, I was not surprised. I had hoped that somehow such a thing would happen. Before going home, I begged him not to repeat it. If the nuns saw us we could not meet again, and our future was already so uncertain. If we really fell in love and then never saw one another again, it would take us a long time to get over it and forget.

The future was uncertain indeed, and the news was not good. Worst of all, from our point of view, had been the occupation of Parma by the SS. The only real Italian resistance had come from the 370 officer pupils of the School of Infantry, who were stationed in a building in the Giardino Pubblico. These and the 33rd Armoured Regiment, whose tanks were no match for those of a German Panzer division, did their best, but it was hopeless. Within four hours it was all over, and the following morning thousands of officers and men found themselves incarcerated in the Cittadella, the great sixteenth-century fortress built by the Farnese on the outskirts of the city. So began 600 days of German occupation.

I was now afraid for Eric and his safety, not just because he was a young man far from home, but also because I was in love with him. I was so worried that one evening I went to see Dr Sambataro. Keeping my feelings hidden from him as well as I could, I suggested that the hospital was becoming too obvious and dangerous a hiding place. The doctor agreed. He had already been involved in taking prisoners to the mountains and told me that he would now have to think of a way to get Eric there too. It would have to be done very soon.

I went to see Eric to tell him about this conversation and found that he had come to the same conclusion. He too was worried; not for himself because he, as a prisoner-of-war, was protected by the Geneva Convention, but for the nuns and me and everyone else with whom he had come into contact.

But the Germans were quicker than any of us. Somehow

they had found out that there was a prisoner in the hospital and Eric suddenly found himself with a guard of three *carabinieri* who were ordered to watch over him night and day and never let him out of their sight until arrangements could be made to send him to Germany. By the following morning my father and the doctor had made a plan for his escape.

At ten o'clock that same night, while Suor Eusebia was engaging the *carabinieri* in conversation, he would have to get out of one of the upper windows of the building and slide down a drainpipe. Still in his pyjamas and with his foot in plaster, he would hobble 500 metres or so across some fields until he reached a track, then carry on for another 500 metres or so until he reached a proper road. There he would be met by the doctor and my father, who was allowed to travel with him because he had regularly accompanied the doctor on his evening rounds before the curfew was established. They would bring with them a set of civilian clothes and, most important, Eric's boots.

That morning I went to the hospital with the excuse of visiting an old woman who was a patient, and while I was there I met one of the *carabinieri* in the corridor. I knew him because he had been in Fontanellato for some months, and after wishing him *buon giorno* and so forth I tried to find out what his duties were and what was likely to happen to the prisoner.

'I don't know; we are here to guard him to prevent him escaping.'

'And if he tries to escape, what are your orders?'

'We have to shoot.'

I went to see Suor Eusebia and gave her a message to deliver to Eric when the attention of the *carabinieri* was elsewhere. It contained all the instructions for his escape that night. I didn't need to tell her to be careful.

Then I waited for the evening to come, but the hours

passed very slowly. After supper my father went to see the doctor and they went for a walk together to kill time up until the appointed hour. Our house was less than a kilometre from the pick-up point. Just before ten o'clock, in the stillness of the night, I heard the noise of a motor car: it could only have been the doctor's.

My mother and I were in the garden. Neither of us spoke but we both knew that if we heard shots it meant that the operation had failed. Eric would perhaps have been killed or wounded and the suspicious position of the car might well have been noticed by somebody. Time stood still; I was full of fear and empty of any other sensation. I could not even say a prayer.

The engine of the car stopped and the doctor and my father were clearly waiting. After what seemed an eternity the engine was restarted and gradually faded away into the night. There had been no shooting.

When my father eventually returned home he was smiling. 'Eric was late,' he said, 'but we were prepared for that and we waited. He escaped in his pyjamas, and the plaster of Paris on his leg was sopping wet where he had fallen in a ditch, but he was in good spirits. What a sight he was!' Neither my father nor the doctor knew the details of how he had escaped. We would have to wait until the following day to hear about them from Suor Eusebia.

Once Eric was in the car they had driven towards Soragna, then by a roundabout route to a big plantation of poplars near the right bank of the Po, where they had directed him to a well-hidden place in the middle. They gave him clothing (which included a black jacket and striped trousers – my father's best suit) and enough food and water to last him until morning. It had been arranged that a trustworthy man would come then to collect him and take him to a safe house. From there, if and when it became possible, he would be taken to the castle at Soragna where the Principessa Meli Lupi was prepared to take him on in the guise of a gardener – a refugee who had been rendered deaf and dumb in the bombing of Milan. (This plan was abandoned when rumours began to circulate that the castle was about to be taken over as a headquarters for Field Marshal Kesselring; rumours which subsequently proved to have no basis in fact.)

On the way to Eric's first hiding place there had been an uncomfortable few minutes when the doctor's car, in spite of its prominently displayed red cross, had been stopped by a *carabinieri* patrol. There had just been time to push Eric to the floor in the back. Fortunately the patrol recognized the doctor and my father, and after learning that the doctor had been called out to visit a seriously ill patient, the men saluted and disappeared into the darkness.

The next morning all Fontanellato knew about the escape. There were many theories about how it had been carried out and who had been the accomplices. Some people ventured to say that Suor Eusebia was one of them, but as everybody had such a very high regard for her they did not pursue the matter further. Few, if any, suspected the doctor or my father of being involved; or if they did they did not say so.

That morning I took time off from the bank to visit Suor Eusebia, who told me exactly what had happened before Eric's escape. After delivering my message to him under a plate on his dinner tray she had gone outside to sit under the tree in the warm evening air. Later she invited the *carabinieri* for a glass of wine and a chat, but only one of them would come. The second insisted on remaining upstairs to guard the prisoner, and the third was off duty, asleep somewhere downstairs.

Earlier in the day Eric had begun to fake a bad stomach-ache and made long and numerous trips to the lavatory. The first few times the *carabiniere* on duty became impatient and tried to make him come out, but the only answer he got was that the prisoner was feeling extremely unwell and wanted please to be left alone. Eventually the *carabiniere* got bored and let Eric stay in the lavatory for as long as he wanted. But in the evening, on what was to prove his last visit, the prisoner was so long and so quiet that eventually the *carabiniere* who had remained to guard him banged on the door. Receiving no reply, he went to call his companion, who was downstairs under the tree with Suor Eusebia. Together, now very alarmed, they prepared to break down the door. At this point Suor Eusebia intervened and told them that she knew how to open it. And she did; but the *Inglese* had disappeared through the window and down a drainpipe.

The two *carabinieri* panicked. They realized they would be severely punished when the Germans learned that they had failed to do their duty. It was Suor Eusebia who eventually persuaded them to put off reporting the escape until the following morning in the faint hope that some excuse might present itself.

In fact they were saved by a chance in a million. Early the following morning a British soldier who had been in the orphanage was admitted to the hospital suffering from a high fever, so the *carabinieri* still had one English prisoner to guard. (Apparently he too managed to escape, on his way to Germany.)

The atmosphere in Fontanellato and the surrounding villages was now very tense. Everyone knew that there were still a lot of prisoners in the surrounding country; but only relatively few, those who were not Fascists, knew exactly where they were. Those who did know had to be careful not to speak because it was only too easy to compromise the families on whose land or in whose houses the prisoners were. It had once been possible to trust a few Fascist families, especially those who had sons who had deserted from the army on 8

September; but that was changing. A number of them – old, dedicated members of the Party who had joined when Mussolini first came to power – fraternized much too much with the Germans. Up to now they had kept a low profile, but they were becoming more militant.

On 21 September, the radio announced that Mussolini, who had been held prisoner in a mountain refuge on the Gran Sasso, in the Abruzzi, had been unexpectedly rescued by German parachutists and taken to Germany. A few days later the Germans launched a strong counter-attack near Salerno where the Allies had landed.

On the second day after Eric's escape, early in the morning, a troop of Germans, accompanied by Fascists, arrived in Fontanellato to look for escaped prisoners. They questioned a lot of people, especially the women, each one of whom put on an innocent face and answered:

'We don't know. People say that they have gone to Switzerland. We haven't seen them in the village. After all, we couldn't feed them as we don't have enough to eat ourselves.'

Becoming angry in the face of this reception, the Germans started what subsequently became known as a *rastrellamento*, which literally means a raking – a detailed search of the area. That day they surrounded the farmhouse of the Baruffini family, where they found several prisoners. Signor Baruffini and another farmer were sent to Germany: both of them died in Mathausen. And altogether, thirteen prisoners-of-war were recaptured that day. All this happened because one of the escaped officers had kept a diary in which he wrote down the names of everyone who had helped him. I was lucky enough not to be on his list, but it was widely believed that there were more arrests to come.

Although the house in which Eric was now hidden was an isolated one, we couldn't exclude the possibility of a German search, so I set off there on my bicycle while the Germans were still questioning people. I knew the paths well and it was a journey of a few kilometres as the crow flies or, as they say in Italy, *a volo d'uccello*.

In our part of Italy, as in every other, there was an information system always in operation: *radio popolo*, the people's radio (what is known in some countries as the grapevine). It brings the latest news, day and night, and seems omniscient. Who knows where it originates? It is always mysterious and secret. That day, by way of the *radio popolo* the news of the *rastrellamento* spread like wildfire, but it had not spread as far as Eric's farm. When I told the farmer what was happening he immediately went off to find Eric, who was hiding in the wood.

'I have to be quick,' I told Eric, and explained why he would not be able to be the Principessa's gardener. 'Personally,' I said, trying to be funny when I didn't feel very funny, 'I think she's had a lucky escape.' I told him that when I had last seen the doctor he had said the situation here in the plain was so serious that Eric would now have to make the choice of going either to Switzerland or to the mountains. If he decided on the mountains the doctor would take him there in his car. It was far too dangerous to remain where he was, not only for him but for everyone else as well.

The farmer left us briefly. We looked at each other, not saying a word, and tears came into my eyes. Eric put his arms round me and held me tight until we heard the farmer coming back. He didn't want to go to Switzerland: if he did go, the chances were that he would be interned there for the rest of the war. In the mountains, as soon as his ankle was mended, he could set off to walk south and try to cross the enemy lines. It was agreed that until the doctor had decided when they should go, Eric would be hidden in a hole in the ground which would be covered with planks and earth –

sufficiently far from the farm for no one to be able to accuse the farmer of having hidden him.

I couldn't stay with him any longer: there was no more time. The farmer stood silently by as we said our farewells. We didn't know if we would ever see each other again.

As soon as I got back to Fontanellato I went to see the doctor, who decided to take Eric to the Apennines the following day. He asked me to try and get him a map but this was a difficult thing to do in a place the size of Fontanellato, where hardly anyone possessed even an atlas of the world. My father had an atlas which had been published in the time of the Austro-Hungarian Empire, but this was on such a small scale that it was virtually useless. Eventually I managed to find a page torn from a local bus timetable which showed the Province of Parma. It was better than nothing, but only just.

A verbal message was sent to the farm: the doctor would arrive at 1 p.m. to pick Eric up on a rough track not far from his underground hiding place. My father was not going with the doctor because the operation would have much less chance of success if they were stopped on the way. The Geneva Convention might protect Eric. It certainly wouldn't protect Italian civilians, particularly not schoolmasters, or even doctors claiming immunity under a red cross.

That day, as we waited for the doctor to come back from the mountains, was one of deep anxiety for the whole family. I went to the Santuario, lit a candle to Our Lady of the Holy Rosary – an act that every Fontanellatese performs when in need of comfort or help – and prayed hard. Towards evening I went to the doctor's house to wait for him. Darkness had fallen long since when, with enormous relief, I saw his car entering the drive.

'I decided to travel to Parma on the Via Emilia,' he told me. 'The back roads are so bad for my tyres, and once these are finished, I'll never get another set. I joined it at Sanguinaro, where I was held up by a *Feldgendarm* on a motorcycle. Eric was sitting in the front looking absurdly English and in the back was an old man I was taking back to the mountains. I thought this must be the end for all three of us but in fact all the policeman wanted to do was to stop any traffic going on to the Via Emilia as a big convoy was on its way south towards Parma. In the end, when he saw the red crosses, he let us go.

'The convoy turned out to be reinforcements for a Panzer division. It was a help to us because all other traffic had been halted in both directions and we were able to race along on the wrong side of the road. I know that Eric was interested in seeing a Panzer division on the move and being so close to the enemy but I could see him getting paler and paler, probably at the thought of what would happen if we were stopped.

'When we got to Parma the car [which worked on methane gas] broke down in the middle of Piazza Garibaldi, which had been completely cleared of civilians because the convoy was going to pass through it. The only other people there were a couple of *Feldgendarmen* and one or two German officers. We had a difficult job starting the car. It had to be done very quickly because once the tanks arrived we would not be allowed to go any further until they had passed through the city.

'Eventually we got to Lagrimone, a little place between Langhirano and Monchio on the way to the Passo di Lagastrello, where I know a family. They promised to look after Eric. When we parted I told Eric that one day soon I would bring you to see him but he was horrified at the idea. He said it would be much too dangerous.'

*

Of the hundreds of prisoners who had escaped from the orphanage there were still a number hidden in the surrounding countryside, but I did not know where. Some reached Switzerland and some made for the mountains, but the majority, around eighty, were recaptured by the Germans. We knew from listening to the Allied radio that groups of *partigiani*, partisans, had secretly started to organize themselves, and young men of military age were advised to go into hiding to avoid being sent to Germany or conscripted. By now the Germans were everywhere: on the Via Emilia, on the Strada della Cisa, which was a vital route of communication across the Apennines into Tuscany, and in the provinces of Parma, Reggio Emilia and Bologna, where there was a division of the Wehrmacht about 20,000 strong.

In late September, soon after Mussolini's escape to Germany, the *Standortkommandantur* on Piazza Garibaldi announced that there would be a reward of 1800 lire – then approximately the equivalent of £25 sterling – for every prisoner-of-war denounced to the authorities.

At about the same time the papers began to acknowledge the existence of the *mercato nero*, the black market, in bread, butter, pasta and other rationed goods (it had always flourished, especially in the Po valley). On 10 November large numbers of passengers from Brescia engaged in the black market were arrested on Parma station.

On 24 November a macabre advertisement appeared in the *Gazzetta di Parma*, inserted by the Todt Organization:

> *Workers in Germany*
> *Find guaranteed work. Good living conditions and equal*
> *rights with German Workers.*

I didn't know of anybody who volunteered. Life in Parma still appeared, on the surface, to be reasonably normal. The Teatro Regio, its name changed to the Teatro Nazionale

Verdi in an attempt to obliterate the memory of royalty, continued to put on operas such as *Otello, Rigoletto, La Traviata* and *Madame Butterfly*.

If anyone can be said to have had a 'finest hour' – although in this instance it was more a matter of finest days and weeks – it was the people of Fontanellato, and those for many miles around, who had showed such courage in helping the escaped prisoners without any hope or thought of recompense. It was now the turn of the mountain people to show the stuff they were made of.

As the weeks passed, far from forgetting our brief time together, I realized how much I missed Eric and wondered where he was and what he was doing. Would we have heard, down here in the *pianura*, if he had been recaptured or killed? The Germans had recaptured a number of prisoners, according to the *Gazzetta di Parma*, but no names were ever published. We had no means of communication with the people in the mountains, which to us were as remote as Tibet, and the doctor had not ventured there again; in fact he was now in great danger. Any sort of travel, even by bus, had become very difficult, and a permit was needed for most journeys from one place to another.

One Sunday when I was attending Mass in the Santuario, I noticed two girls in the next pew who were wearing greased mountain boots and thick hand-knitted socks. I had never seen them before and they obviously came from some very rural place in the Apennines. I could not resist asking them where they came from, as at that time of the year there were very few pilgrims about. They told me that they came from the country near Lagrimone and that they had obtained permission to come to pray in the Santuario for their cousin who was fighting in Russia. This was just an excuse: the real reason they wanted to come was that they very much needed food at home. Near Fontanellato they had a cousin who

148

owned a *caseificio* and had promised to give them some butter and cheese. I looked at them. They seemed sincere and genuine.

'Have you heard of a prisoner called Enrico?' I asked, trying to hide my excitement. They had not, they said, but they had a lot of reliable relatives and could easily find out where he was and deliver any message I wanted to send him, if he was there. If not, the message could be burned.

As they were not leaving the church immediately I rushed home and quickly wrote a note to 'la Signora Enrica' telling Eric all the latest news and telling him also how lonely I was without him. In the darkness of the church – there were only a few old women praying, oblivious of what went on around them – one of the girls took the note and quickly hid it in her knickers.

As the autumn advanced, food began to be short even in the Po valley, for the farmers and the owners of the *caseifici* had to declare to the authorities what they were producing. From time to time we still had meat, for cattle still had to be slaughtered and there was little transport, because of the fuel shortage, to carry them to the wholesale market. The meat was often sold on stalls in the villages, but there was a limit to what one could buy. Families had no freezers and very few had fridges, so what was bought had to be consumed almost immediately. Even Signor Grignaffini with his big stomach could only eat a certain amount at one time.

I continued to work in the bank and give private lessons at weekends. There were no more dances in the *balere* to distract me; partly because it was difficult to move freely from one village to another and partly because the evening curfew still applied. I started giving lessons to more pupils, which sometimes involved cycling to houses far out in the country-side.

There was a village near ours called Fontevivo which,

having a number of oil and methane-gas plants, became a target for the Allied air-forces. The first bombing was at Bianconese, very near Fontevivo, and it took place at the end of September 1943. We in Fontanellato were not afraid because we thought that apart from houses and farms we had nothing worth bombing. We forgot that the castle was now a German headquarters and that the orphanage had become a school for officer cadets of the resurgent Fascist Party. These cadets were all young and highly dedicated: the hated Repubblichini.

The Repubblichini seemed to have settled in well in Fontanellato. They tried to be friendly; they frequented the cafés and even ventured into people's houses, and they didn't seem to do any harm. Some of them came to our house on some pretext or other, but they met with a chilly reception from my mother, who could look severe and forbidding when she wanted to. Whatever we may have felt, however, we had to be careful not to show too much dislike, because the Repubblichini were gaining strength all the time.

The atmosphere in the villages was one of suspense and distrust. How would everything end? My father and the doctor felt worried and insecure. The newspapers were full of propaganda and of distorted news of 'traitors' to the regime and the country. Reports of the Allied advance in southern Italy were much played down. On 28 October, the anniversary of the Fascists' ascent to power, the *Gazzetta di Parma* had proclaimed: 'Led by the genius of Mussolini, Italy greets the fated date with unshakable certainty of victory.'

At around the same time Colonel Stephens started to broadcast news from London. He had a vast clandestine audience. Very early each morning, which we thought was a fairly safe time to listen, we sat glued to the radio.

We had recently begun to shelter a young man who had deserted from the Italian army in the south and had somehow

150

managed, with the help of various Italians whom he met on the way, to reach Fontanellato. He was a Slovene from Zadar and spoke perfect Italian. In the village he was told to come to us because we came from Yugoslavia too. My mother took pity on him and agreed to keep him for as long as she could. He would have to be very careful, only going out after dusk when he could do some jobs for other people in exchange for a little food. Bruno was tall and naturally pale; more so now because he was also very frightened. He was an artist and his only dream was one day to go back home and paint. He only felt secure in his bed, which he found beautifully warm because every night my mother would place between the sheets the *prete*, an iron pot full of hot ashes; it had a framework of wood to stop the bedding catching fire. Bruno felt perfectly happy in that bed; he seemed to forget all his worries.

Even he, who loved his bed more than anything, joined us to listen to Colonel Stephens, and when news came of some successful advance against the Axis he would burst into wonderful, joyous laughter.

It was on a rather cold morning at the end of October, just before breakfast, that we heard footsteps on the stairs outside our flat. There was a knock on the door, an unusual thing at that hour of the morning. Fortunately we had the presence of mind to turn the radio on to another station before opening the door.

Two tall men entered without bothering to ask for permission. They were dressed in long dark raincoats and wore dark felt hats and they addressed themselves to my father, ignoring the rest of us. I will remember their sinister looks and cold eyes until I die. When I look at Elizabeth Frink's terrifying bronze thugs of the 1960s I am always reminded of those men: members of the Fascist Secret Police. 'Signor Skof, we would like you to come with us to the barracks to answer

151

some questions,' one of them said; and the other: 'You will be allowed home this afternoon.' He did not make any attempt to eliminate from his voice his complete disbelief in what he was saying. They looked at the radio, as if it would tell them something, and then their cold eyes settled on Bruno, who was not laughing any more. In fact he was trembling like a leaf, but they didn't seem to notice.

'Who is he?' the first man asked. 'We have no information about any sons.' My mother was quick: 'He is the butcher's boy. He has only come to see if we want any meat, which will be coming into the shop tomorrow. It's a cold morning and I was going to give him a cup of coffee.' Whether they believed this or not, it was impossible to say. They simply told my father to hurry up and put his jacket on. They repeated that he didn't need anything else because he would be back in the afternoon, which more than anything else they could have said made me wonder if we would ever see him again.

Without another word they took him away. Tears came to my eyes and to Bruno's, but my mother put on a brave face. 'This is no time for crying,' she told me firmly. 'Viktor has not done anything wrong. He will be back. You will see. I will go to the Santuario and pray. You go and explain to the manager of the bank what has happened and tell him that you won't be able to go to work this morning. And you, Bruno, cannot remain here a moment longer. I will ask a family I know well, out in the country, if you can stay with them.'

Midday came but there was no news. I went to the barracks, the *caserma*, in Fontanellato to find out when my father was going to be released, but was told that they did not know, for he was in the hands of the Secret Police. Back home, I did not tell my mother this; it seemed better to wait. One could hear every 'tick-tock' of the clock, but the hours seemed never to pass. I went for news again and this time was told that both my father and Dr Sambataro had been taken to the San Francesco Prison, a civilian prison in Parma.

That evening my mother and I felt vulnerable and very much alone, uncertain what steps to take. We did not know any influential person in Parma who could help us, and certainly there was no one in Fontanellato. We cried until suddenly my mother said, 'We will not achieve anything with tears. Sing and try to have a good night's sleep. Your father is innocent. God will help him.' And so we sang.

The next morning I telephoned the prison. Yes, I was told, they had somebody of the name of Skof. One member of his family could come and visit him that afternoon and yes, we would be allowed to bring food, which would be examined before being given to the prisoner.

I persuaded my mother that I should be the first visitor; after all, I knew Parma better than she did, and since I was a young girl they might treat me more kindly. The people's radio started to work immediately: in no time friends began bringing us gifts of food and wine for my father.

I went to the prison. I had never been in one before. I felt terribly alone. I told the guard at the reception desk in the dark, grim entrance why I had come and he told me to wait. It was fortunate that I had a little time to accustom myself to being in such a place and to the thought of seeing my father. I had to put on a brave face and try to show him that I was not worried, but when he appeared I was shocked at how much he had changed even in such a short time. He was unshaven and looked terribly pale. He said he was not treated badly and that he was with other political prisoners. There was nothing for him to do but play cards, which was allowed. I told him, although it was not true, that the local *carabinieri* had said he would not remain locked up there for long, but I am sure he did not believe me.

153

In the following days and weeks my mother and I took turns to visit him every day; we realized how much our presence meant to him. We were seriously worried, for he was neither young nor fit, and his morale was terribly low. Sometimes we took food for Dr Sambataro too, as his wife was not well and could not go often, but we were never allowed to see him.

My mother and I were terrified that my father would be picked out of the prison and shot. One early morning a friend came to tell us that two dead men had been left in the cemetery during the night. He hadn't seen them and didn't know who they were. As there was a curfew nobody knew who had brought them there either. I believe that courage is sometimes born out of despair. Before our friend had finished telling us his news I got on my bicycle and rode to the cemetery as fast as I could. There were already people there. With a heart beating as if it wanted to explode I looked at the two dead men; I had never seen either of them before.

One day, as I was waiting to be admitted to the prison, I heard quite a young man talking to the guard in broken but familiar Italian: it sounded like Triestino. Could he have been from the border of Italy and Yugoslavia? I plucked up my courage and asked him. 'Yes,' he said. 'You are right.' He was a Slovene called Vlado from near Ljubljana, attached to the German Army; and as he spoke fluent German he was acting as an interpreter. 'And why are you here?' he asked. I told him about my family and where they came from, then told him about my father. He shook his head.

'You probably don't know,' he said, 'but the Germans have no plans for the political prisoners. They simply keep them as hostages. If a German soldier is killed by the partisans or by civilians, they take a certain number of political prisoners out and shoot them.'

He saw the look of horror on my face. 'Don't be upset; I

will try to help you if I can. But there is something I want to ask you. I know the name Skof. Was your mother ever a refugee in Yugoslavia during the 1914–18 war? Have you ever heard of a place called Ribnica?'

'Yes,' I said. 'She often talked about it and about the kindness of the family who gave her a room. In fact she talked so much and so often about it that I feel I have been there myself.'

'Was her name Gizela and her son's Slavko?'

'Yes,' I replied, and could not say any more. It was such an unbelievable coincidence.

He told me how well he remembered my mother as a refugee in his home and how much his parents and grand-father had liked her and thought of her as part of the family. He said that they had never forgotten her; nor had he forgotten Slavko, with whom he used to play. He paused and thought for a moment, obviously very moved. Then he told me to wait for him after I had visited my father, and said that he would try to think of a way to help me without arousing any suspicion.

When I came back from my visit he was there in the entrance, waiting.

'Listen carefully, I have to be brief,' he said. 'There is an important German headquarters in the suburbs of the town. It is in a villa which you will easily find because it is near the river. It is part of the *Militarkommandantur*. This is the address. I can't actually give it to you because it will arouse suspicion from the guard. Just read it now, remember it, and then destroy it. In two days' time you must appear there. I myself have to go there with one of the officers from the prison, to interpret. I will make sure that I meet you but I shall pretend that I have never seen you before. You must ask for the Kommandant. I shall go to him to tell him that you want to speak to him personally and do not want to tell anybody else the reason. As I shall be the only interpreter there I shall have to be present. He will ask you questions. You can reply as you wish but I shall translate in whatever way I think appropriate. Good luck.'

Back at home I told my mother of this extraordinary encounter. She found it hard to believe that such a thing had happened, and tears came to her eyes. She well remembered the little Vlado. He had been about four years old, and although he was younger than my brother, they always got on very well together and were heartbroken when the time came for them to part.

On the appointed day I presented myself at the villa. It had only a very small, hardly noticeable brass plate outside which gave nothing away. I rang the bell, and the door was opened by a German in army uniform.

'*Sprechen Kommandant, bitte, privaten,*' I said very slowly, as if I had just learned these words and found difficulty in repeating them. He told me to wait, but soon I was ushered into an office with an enormous map of Parma Province on the wall, and a senior officer in uniform sitting at the desk. He asked me in German what I had come for but I said; untruthfully, '*Nicht verstehen.*' He called the interpreter, who gave no sign that he had ever seen me before, and began asking me questions. I felt terrified but I managed to control myself. It didn't matter what I answered because Vlado, according to plan, translated as he thought fit. I was asked why I had come about my father, why he was in prison, and many other questions. I answered in Italian that my father had been an officer in the Austrian army and that he spoke good German. And I asked for the Kommandant's help to have him released.

The Kommandant made a number of telephone calls and then, to my complete surprise, said that my father would be home the following evening. He added that in return I had to help him: I would have to come to his office once a week and report on what was happening in Fontanellato. In this I must not fail. I agreed; I hadn't much choice. Vlado told me that I must do as he asked – but I could simply make myself appear a fool by reporting news of no consequence. (There was in truth not much happening in Fontanellato at this time, and although we heard news of the partisans we never knew where they were.)

The next evening my father was brought home in a German car, but he seemed a broken man. They had not ill-treated him in prison, but the fact that his future had been so very much in danger had had a tremendous influence on his morale. It took him a long time to recover. And Dr Sambataro was still in prison.

For the next few weeks I reported my unimportant news to the office. I was eventually told to appear once a fortnight and later relieved from my duty altogether, probably because the senior officer I reported to was replaced. Two weeks after my father's release Dr Sambataro, faking appendicitis, was taken from the prison to the hospital in Parma, where the surgeons supported him in his pretence. He remained there for some time. Eventually he managed to escape from the hospital and spent the rest of the war in the mountains with the partisans.

Amid all these shattering events I had little time to try to find out what had happened to Eric. I knew more or less where he was and I knew he had not been recaptured – that was all. Then suddenly the chance came to visit him. I was able to let him know in advance of my possible visit by giving a short letter to someone in Fontanellato, a patient of Dr Sambataro's, who was going to visit a very ill relative in Lagrimone. I told Eric to expect me; somehow I would let him know the date by way of one of the *contadini* who were helping him.

With some difficulty I managed to get a permit to travel

from Parma in a bus which went up into the hills to Lagrimone; once there, I would walk to the house of a Signor Ugolotti,* some distance from the village.

The family received me very warmly and Signora Ugolotti insisted that I should have something to eat: white coffee made with acorns, and home-made bread. I had to be quick, they told me; it was quite a long climb to the hut where Eric would be waiting and I had to return to Parma that night. It would be dark long before then, because the sky was full of clouds and it was raining. I felt terribly excited. How would I find him? Would he be happy to see me?

Signor Ugolotti led the way up through the dense woods. I walked silently, testing every step I took on the rough paths, just as I had used to walk with my mother in the woods near Štanjel. When we finally reached the hut where Eric was supposed to be, it was deserted. We went inside and waited: the minutes seemed like hours. Eventually we saw a figure coming slowly towards us, clearly visible because the sky, as if by a miracle, had started to clear and a brilliant moon had appeared. As he came nearer I could see that he was wearing a velveteen suit which was full of holes and splattered with wet clay. It was Eric. We looked at each other without words and formally embraced; to my surprise Eric embraced Signor Ugolotti too. Then, obviously wanting to leave us alone, our friend said that he had to go to the village of Lalatta for a short time; he would be back in twenty minutes, by which time I would have to start making my way back to Lagrimone.

I was glad of these few minutes alone with Eric. I told him about my father's arrest; about the doctor; about life in Fontanellato; about the *mercato nero*; about the Allies being stuck between Rome and Naples; about the bombing of the cities, especially Genoa. He told me about himself and where

* Eric invented the names Zannoni (for Ugolotti) and James (for Donald) for his book *Love and War in the Apennines*.

he was staying and about how people treated him. Before I left I was able to give him the good news about his friend Donald,* one of the officers to whom we had given food and clothes on the banks of the Rovacchia. The doctor had wanted to bring him here but was not very happy about making the same journey twice, so he had taken him to the next valley. No doubt James would visit Eric soon, for he had been told where he was. Lastly I told him that there was supposed to be a plan for a British submarine which would take off escaped prisoners somewhere near La Spezia, and I produced some maps of the area which I had managed to get from a bookseller friend of mine in Parma. I was not very optimistic about the submarine and neither was Eric. Then Signor Ugolotti appeared: it was time to go. We parted with a kiss and Eric said, 'God bless you.'

I gave him a parcel of food and clothes wrapped in newspaper and left the hut without turning back.

On 29 December I read in the *Gazzetta di Parma* the news that Eric – and Donald – had been recaptured. Eric's name was not given but it was not difficult to guess that it was him. He had been interrogated at the Comando di Legione in Parma before being locked up in the Citadella to await removal to Germany. Would he emerge alive? Would any of us? Deep in my heart there was still hope that one day I would receive a letter saying, 'I am alive and I have not forgotten you.' And it was this that kept me going.

That winter there was another sinister addition to the Germans and the Repubblichini in Fontanellato: Mongols – a people we had heard of but had never seen – who had been taken prisoner on the Russian front and were now attached to the German army. They carried no arms but were said to obey the most savage orders without showing any emotion.

* See footnote on page 158

They settled in an empty building with a German officer in charge of them. It was rumoured that they had already burned farms in other villages, so their mere presence filled the Fontanellatesi with terror.

One day, returning home, I found my mother outside our front door, surrounded by four of them. My heart stopped beating; what was happening? What were they going to do to us? But to my surprise I saw, as I got near them, that they all had broad smiles on their faces and were showing my mother photographs of their families. She, speaking Slovene, had managed to understand their primitive Russian, and they were delighted to have found a civilian who was able to communicate with them a little, and who reminded them of their mothers.

'Poor people,' said my mother after they had gone. 'They are terribly homesick being so far away from their families and their country. I gave them a cup of *Ruski čaj* [Russian tea], and that made them very, very happy.'

The Mongols stayed in Fontanellato for a few weeks and did no harm to anybody. They went as they had appeared, at night.

It was in the spring of 1944 that we in Fontanellato began to feel what war was all about. Food was beginning to be in seriously short supply, the black market was flourishing ever more strongly, new orders and threats emanated continually from the Germans, and Allied air raids were frequent. While the Germans were fighting on enormously wide fronts in Russia and in Italy, the Allies were advancing from the south. In advancing, they made northern Italy the target for their big day- and night-bombing attacks. The first large-scale one near us was on Milan. Several times, late in the evening, we saw the whole northern sky illuminated by flares and heard the heavy, terrible rumblings of bombardment, although the city was 100 kilometres away. On nights like this all Fontanellato was out, defying the curfew, and we all prayed that it would soon end and prayed for the people who lived there.

On 23 April the bombing came much nearer. In two big raids the wings of Maria Luigia's Palazzo Ducale, occupied by the Guardia Nazionale Repubblicana, were destroyed. Up to that time Parma had not been touched, and the Parmigiani had lived in the irrational hope that the Americans would not bomb the city because Toscanini, by then living in the United States, had persuaded them not to do so. After the bombing, virulent attacks on Toscanini appeared in the *Gazzetta di Parma*. The Parmigiani had also hoped that their city would not be attacked because it was *rossa* – red – and therefore theoretically immune.

Later in April, American Flying Fortresses badly damaged Piazza Garibaldi, the Teatro Regio and the Pilotta, the great palace of the Farnese, and – a terrible loss – destroyed the Teatro Farnese, a beautiful, unique, all-wooden theatre. Many other important buildings were also razed to the ground.

The Madonna had apparently decided not to protect Fontanellato either. We suffered three air raids. The first was in March, when eight bombs fell on the outskirts of the village, killing one person and wounding fourteen others, and damaging the convent in which the Dominican nuns lived. I was working in the bank, trying to close the accounts for the day, when the first bomb fell. I didn't realize what had happened until the second bomb followed it. I was petrified, but there was nothing I could do. I was in sole charge of the bank, and I was responsible for the safe and its contents because the Manager had gone to Parma that day. I couldn't go out and leave everything unattended, so I remained and waited for what I thought must be the end. Having discharged their bombs, the planes left. They returned weeks later to make more raids and claim more lives.

Life in Fontanellato was certainly not dull: there were plenty of people about, even if we had no cinema and there were no dances. The parties I missed most were the ones in Valeria's house. Unfortunately her family lived under a constant cloud of danger. Her mother, being Jewish, had to keep well out of sight and didn't venture out. She didn't even want people to know that she was living there. If there was any sign of a *rastrellamento* in the neighbouring villages or in our own, a *carabiniere* who was a friend of the family used to cycle over and warn her. She would then go into a secret hiding place that only her family knew about.

That same spring I received a letter from my aunt in Mavhinje telling me that the village had been burned to the ground. Most of the men who had not joined the partisans had been deported to Germany and most of the young women had been sent to work in factories in the Reich. Among these was my cousin Zdenka. My aunt didn't get many letters from her, and those she did get were censored, but from the way Zdenka wrote, it was obvious that she was very hungry. In Mavhinje there was hardly any food and it was difficult to send parcels. She gave me Zdenka's German address and asked if I could at least write to her daughter from time to time to keep her spirits up. 'We haven't got much,' my mother said when she read the letter, 'but we've certainly got more than she or the other people in Mavhinje have. If we can find a way of sending a parcel, we must do so. Poor girl, she can't work and not eat.'

I had an idea. Could I not go to the castle where the German headquarters were and ask if they could forward a small gift of food to a worker in Germany? Surely they wouldn't refuse. I went to the castle and was asked to wait in a comfortable room. I had not been there long when an officer appeared, shook my hand and asked if he could help me in any way. When I explained the purpose of my visit, he answered with a smile: 'But of course, there is no objection to your sending the parcel or parcels with our mail. It goes every day and I can assure you that your cousin who is helping Germany to victory with her work will receive them very quickly.'

Not only did she receive them quickly, but her answers arrived back in no time. We continued to send parcels as often as we could.

My father, now free and teaching as usual, felt less and less safe. So when he was asked to act as a German–Italian interpreter whenever soldiers or officers appeared in the village, he could only agree. The Fontanellatesi knew where his real sympathies lay, and they knew that he could not refuse to do as he was asked.

Now that the partisans were well organized in the Province of Parma they committed many acts of sabotage. At times, too, they shot Germans, even in the city, which inevitably led to savage repercussions. There were five formations of partisans strategically placed in the province, each with its own duties. Each formation consisted of no more than fifty men, and they were no longer called *ribelli*, rebels, but went by the name of their commandant. The Germans were extremely worried about the organization, and ordered all young Italian men born in 1923, 1924 and 1925 to present themselves at various barracks within fifteen days. They also declared that anybody who was helping the 'rebels' would be shot.

On 27 June Field Marshal Kesselring, whose headquarters were in Sant'Andrea Bagni, a village some fifteen kilometres from Fontanellato, said that he would not tolerate the partisans any more, and three days later he ordered two large-scale *rastrellamenti*. A wide semicircle of Germans and Repubblichini formed on the edge of the *pianura* near Parma and moved up towards the mountains, looting and burning villages; sometimes shooting in the air to spread terror and sometimes

163

hanging or deporting the inhabitants. In the course of these operations they killed and wounded more than 500 people, but even with these drastic measures they did not succeed in doing what they had set out to do. In later *rastrellamenti* the Germans were helped by the Mongols, who were acclimatized to the winter cold. The partisans showed great courage, but some of them had to withdraw from the Parma Apennines down towards Tuscany.

Travelling became very difficult. Transport was scarce and we had to carry special identity cards when we moved from our own villages. It was difficult for our branch of the bank, which was not allowed to keep more than a certain amount of money in the safe, and often had to send documents and money to the head branch in Parma. The post was much too risky, so sometimes I was asked to carry funds to Parma on my bicycle. As I was a young girl no one, partisans or Germans, would suspect me of carrying very large sums of money. And I was fortunate: no one ever stopped me either to ask me for my identity card or to see what I had in my bag.

In June 1944 we heard of the fall of Rome. Some very optimistic people thought that the war would be over in a couple of weeks and these hopes were reinforced when news came of the invasion of Normandy. Now fantastic rumours started to circulate to the effect that the Virgin of Fatima might appear again – her last apparition had been in Portugal on 13 October 1927. Some people claimed to have seen the sun turn in the sky, in the same way as it had when the miracle occurred so many years before. People really began to expect the war to end in August, or at the latest in September. So convinced were the farmers that in July they delayed the *trebbiatura*, the threshing of the grain, hoping that they could do it under Allied administration; they thought they would probably get 700 lire more for each sack.

The partisans too hoped for a quick end. In the city the

Gruppi di Azione Patriottica, the GAP, started to carry out assassinations. Nothing violent happened in Fontanellato because there were no partisans in the village: it was full of Germans and Repubblichini. At home we listened to the official news, which we knew was full of propaganda. The people's radio told us more real news, but these days we were too afraid to listen to Colonel Stephens. 'Lili Marlene' was constantly being moaned out on the radio, but when I was with my friends, the ones who had gramophones, we played American records which their parents had acquired years before the war.

Because we needed food, more and more of my free time was taken up by teaching, even at weekends. One hot afternoon I was cycling on a lonely road to a country house where I had two pupils when I heard a plane buzzing rather low over my head. The Allied pilot seemed intent on me: was it because he liked blondes? I wondered. Suddenly I became a target for this lunatic, and he began to shower me with machine-gun bullets. After a minute or two he made a wide turn and flew towards me once again. I just had time to dive into the nearest ditch, dropping the bicycle on the road, before I heard another shower of bullets. I closed my eyes and invoked the Madonna. When I thought he had finished, I opened them, only to see the plane make a parabola in the sky and dive on me again, firing away furiously in an attempt to eliminate me. After this third attempt the plane disappeared, but I didn't move until I was sure that he had really gone. When I got out of the ditch I felt very shocked, and unable to believe that he had missed me. I cancelled the afternoon's lessons and returned home in a daze, cursing the Allies and hoping that they would be better behaved if they ever came to liberate us.

The Allies seemed to be drawn as if by a magnet to our local villages. Perhaps they suffered from insomnia, because every night, just when everybody was settled in bed, a slow noisy little plane – we called it Pippo – came buzzing around. Here and there Pippo dropped a bomb, but hardly ever on a village; he came out of sheer perversity, we felt, just to rob us of our sleep. During the first few days people left their houses for fear of being bombed by Pippo, but quite soon he became part of our lives and we didn't bother about him any more.

One day in August, three weeks after my adventure with the machine-gunner, I finished work early and went to the Taro for a swim. On my return late in the afternoon I saw two SS soldiers outside our front door. My first thought was that they must have come to ask my father for his help in interpreting. Upstairs another SS man was talking to my mother, who seemed very calm. When he saw me he asked me who I was, then demanded to know where my father was. My mother had already told him that she didn't know the answer to this question. I didn't know it either. He was silent for a moment, then ordered me to go and find my father at once and tell him to return home immediately; and not to forget to return home myself.

As soon as I got out of the house, I was told by our neighbours where my father was hiding, but I realized that if I went to speak to him, some SS soldier might follow me and arrest him. After cycling to various different parts of the village pretending to look for him, therefore, I returned and told the Germans that no one had seen my father; he was probably out in the country on his bicycle but I had no idea where.

The SS man who had told me to find him seemed to be particularly irritated by this information. 'We will find him another time,' he said. 'Now you and your mother will come with us. Just take a small bag with what you need for the night and a warm pullover and leave the key to your door with your next-door neighbours.' Our next-door neighbours, Ada and her parents, were there with us listening, very distressed. We gave them two addresses to which they could write in case we did not return and told them where our more precious belongings were. After that we embraced and, with tears pouring down our cheeks, we were made to go outside, where a lorry was waiting with other villagers in it. We were about to leave for our unknown destination when we heard a well-known voice shouting 'Wait!' in German. It was my father, who had come out of hiding because he didn't want to be parted from us. They took him; and then, as an afterthought, they took my bicycle as well.

It was nearly dark when we left Fontanellato and, with no lights about, it was hard to know where we were going after a few kilometres. The lorry travelled very slowly on the dusty roads. As we began to climb there could be no doubt that our destination was to be some place in the hills. Eventually we arrived at what seemed to be a ghost village: no one was in sight.

The lorry stopped near a church and we were made to get down. The church door was opened and, guarded by the SS, we were told to enter. We were to spend the night here on the floor. Each person was given a blanket, but no food; I suspect the soldiers assumed we had brought some with us. When we were all in, the door was locked from outside; if anybody needed the lavatory, they would have to knock.

Left alone, we began to speculate about where we were and why, and where we would ultimately be taken. Two or three people were almost sure we were in Tabiano Terme, a spa in the hills near Parma. There was a dim light in the church which did not make the atmosphere any jollier. It was still early in the evening and the night was going to be very long. Altogether there were forty of us, all from Fontanellato apart from a shipowner from Genoa who had been spending a

holiday in his house in the country. We wondered how we
had been chosen. Somebody who knew us must have given a
list of our names to the Germans, and it must have been
somebody from Fontanellato. We all knew that the Repubblichini were tools of the Nazis, used as spies and as a police
force; but they did not know us well enough to denounce us
as anti-Fascists. It must have been somebody from the village.
We tried to tell ourselves that it was all some terrible mistake,
and that we would soon be returning home. The Fontanellatesi had a good sense of humour, which helped us to keep up
our morale; one rather large, well-educated lady called Fiora
Gandini was able to make us all laugh. I was the youngest
member of the party, and perhaps because of my youth I had
more hope than the others. I had to try and find out where
we were.

I told my parents that I wanted to go to the lavatory and
have a wash. My parents didn't want to let me go, but I
begged them and promised to come back very quickly. I
knocked on the door and the SS guard opened it and asked
what I wanted. He said that he could not leave his post but
that if I was prepared to wait he would ask somebody else to
escort me. I had to be escorted because the curfew was on
and the village was heavily guarded. I didn't have to wait
long: another soldier passed and was asked to accompany
me. On the way we met two patrols with machine guns and
my escort had to give what I thought was a password. We
arrived at some barracks, which I was told were occupied by
Austrian soldiers. They were very surprised to see a young
girl alone at that time of night. In imperfect German I
explained why I was there. They made me very welcome,
then gave me a clean towel and showed me the showers.
When I had finished I thanked them and was escorted back.
On the way I asked my guard what the name of the village
was.

'Tabiano,' he answered. 'It's a pity we don't ever stay here long – we are constantly sent out on missions. The hills are full of partisans. Recently I have witnessed some terrible things. If we could only stay here longer in this village we could take the cure. We need rest.'

'Where do you think they are going to take us?' I asked.

'I don't know, but to guess from what happened to the people before you, you will be sent to Germany. What I do know is that all you people are here because the Fascists have given the list of your names to our headquarters.'

The future seemed gloomy. We were in their hands and obviously we needed a miracle to get us out. I decided not to tell my parents what I had discovered: I would just confirm that we were in Tabiano. But when I got back I didn't have a chance to tell them anything. I found my mother in tears and my father very angry.

'Where have you been all this time? Are you mad? You don't go out with SS soldiers at this time of night; they might have shot you.' But their relief at having me back was greater than their anger, and all was forgiven. It was difficult to sleep that night, not only because the floor was hard, but because we couldn't escape the worry of what the future had in store for us. From time to time somebody would burst into song or laughter, and some people continued to whisper on and off all through the night.

We woke up early. Some of us needed to go out to the lavatory, and all of us asked for a wash. Two basins were provided, with jugs of water and a few towels. Later, ersatz coffee and bread were brought in. I felt rather quiet. There was no one of my age to whom I could talk, and I didn't want to venture out any more. The hours passed without our receiving any news, and night-time took an eternity to come. Once it was dark our spirits were again surprisingly high; we all felt as if we belonged to a large family. We had an apparently inexhaustible number of jokes, made funnier by the Parmigiano dialect. But why, we all kept on asking, haven't they sent us away yet? On the second morning we woke early once again, and after the coffee had been distributed, an officer entered the church. Our hearts stopped beating; we were about to hear our fate. But the officer was smiling.

'An order has come from headquarters that you are all to be freed this afternoon,' he said. 'A bus will take you back to your village. But as this is a high-security place, you cannot leave the church until you are given the order.'

It was too wonderful to be true; our emotions were indescribable. People wept, and my mother embraced my father; I had never seen her do such a thing before. 'We are free, we are free,' was all we could say. And then everyone burst out singing in praise of the Madonna of Fontanellato:

> Blessed Virgin of Fontanellato
> welcome the humble tribute of your people
> and accept their prayer,
> blessed Virgin.

We all sang it with all our hearts – even those of us who never went to church.

My mind was full of happiness and relief. Then I suddenly remembered that the Germans had taken my bicycle, my most treasured possession. Without a word to anybody, I banged on the door, and asked once again for permission to go and wash. As before, a guard accompanied me to the barracks; but this time, on the way back, we met two officers: it was exactly what I had hoped for. As they came nearer I approached them, before the guard had time to prevent me. They stopped, and the senior officer asked what I wanted.

'Sir,' I replied. 'I was brought up here by your soldiers and now we have been set free. But when they took me they also took my bicycle, and I can't live without it. Please, please can I have it back?'

Surprised, he paused, and gave an order to my guard. 'Rest assured,' he said, 'your bicycle will be returned. It will be difficult to find the exact one as we have confiscated so many; but this soldier who is accompanying you will take you to a warehouse where you will find hundreds of bicycles of all descriptions. Just take the one you like and take a good one; I will authorize it personally. I want you to be happy.'

I thanked him, he saluted, and the two of them walked on. My guard said that I was crazy; I could have run into terrible trouble, but I had been lucky and now I had only to choose a beautiful new bicycle.

'But I don't want a beautiful new bicycle – I want my own one,' I said. By now I didn't care what the soldier thought. My craziness was going to get me my bicycle back and I was going home; I felt immensely happy. We went into the warehouse, which was enormous, and encountered a sea of bicycles – more bicycles than I had ever imagined could possibly exist. Some were new, some were old; some were for men, some for women; some had baskets, some did not. There were rows of them hanging on hooks, and stacks of them leaning against one another on the floor. I was speechless. How could I possibly find mine when there were so many hundreds of them, and so many black ones? As it turned out, all the bicycles were numbered and labelled according to where they came from. Fontanellato bicycles came under *Nummer 1230–9*. My bicycle was there, and it had not been damaged at all.

The soldier, seeing my uninteresting-looking machine, asked me again if I would not prefer to choose a new one, but I refused.

We were taken home that afternoon, and during the journey back we sang all sorts of songs except the Fascist ones. When

171

we finally reached home, many of the Fontanellatesi came out to welcome us. It was an unforgettable moment.

At home we were soon given the answer to a question which had been puzzling us: Who had saved us? And why? The stables of the castle had been bought from the Sanvitale family a few years before by a family from Milan (but of Fontanellato origin) called the Gandini. They had converted them into a fine house, which had been requisitioned by the Germans: the officer in charge was a Captain Foghel who, by the time we were taken to Tabiano, had already been transferred to Bologna. Foghel always behaved correctly in Fontanellato. In the lorry with the rest of us had been five members of the Gandini family, which left one of the sons still free. Fortunately he lost no time. He went to Bologna, saw Foghel, and begged him to help. It was not easy, even for a German captain, to intervene at this stage, but once he had been subjected to a long discussion and much persuasion, he contacted the SS in Tabiano and managed to have us set free.

Now we couldn't be in any doubt that some people were not to be trusted. Among the most dangerous was the Chaplain of the Repubblichini, a Catholic priest whom everybody had suspected for a long time. My father was still forced from time to time to act as an interpreter, but from now on he spent much more time at home, rather than meeting his friends in the cafés for a game of cards. I continued to work in the bank and to give lessons, and did not venture far from the village on my bicycle except on the bank's business.

One day one of the German officers stationed in Fontanellato, an Oberleutnant Bauer, called on me and asked if I could give him Italian lessons. He would come in the evening, after the curfew, when he had finished his duties. I could hardly refuse, but I did refuse to take any payment, although I really needed the money. I asked instead if he would teach me German.

172

He came three times a week, and was very eager to learn. He had taught German literature in the high school in Breslau. He was also very tall and very charming, and he gave me to understand, although he never stated it, that he did not believe in the war or in a German victory. All he wanted was to go back home to his wife and his teaching. He left Fontanellato early the following January, and I received two cards from him written in excellent Italian. Months later, when the war was over, I received a third, with the single word *saluti* written on it. A short note accompanied the card, informing me that it had been found on Oberleutnant Bauer's body. He had been killed in action.

I enjoyed teaching Bauer, because he was an intelligent pupil, because there was a gentle air about him, and because he was very kind to my parents. From time to time he brought them small presents of coffee and sugar, although he was always slightly shy and embarrassed about giving them.

After the Tabiano incident my parents and I didn't feel happy about possessing a radio. We could be accused of listening to foreign propaganda even if we were not, and now that we were on the suspected list this could have been a good excuse for having us arrested again. Could I ask Bauer, I wondered, if he would keep it in his office and give it back to us when he had to leave? In the end this is what I did. He agreed with pleasure, and said that it would be absolutely safe.

Christmas came, and the German officers celebrated it by singing '*Heilige Nacht*' and drinking heavily in the Casa Gandini, which they still occupied. It was a sparkling night. Pippo continued to bother us, though we had long since stopped taking any notice of him, and the Allied air attacks continued.

On 28 December, partisans made repeated attacks on German transport on the Via Emilia, their main line of communication with the battle front, which led to a threat by the

Germans that they would burn the villages along the length of the road. They didn't carry out this threat, but in February the terrible Captain Albert of the Sicherheitsdienst, whose headquarters were in the Via Walter Bianchi in Parma, captured more than twenty partisan leaders after subjecting a number of other captives to agonizing tortures.

It was a bitterly cold winter with thick snow; both sides were bogged down in the Apennines from December to April. By the second half of February the Germans were beginning to be really worried by the advance – although slow – of the Allies and by the strong resistance of the partisans, so they decided to make a deal with the partisan leaders to save their own lives. Through an emissary, they threatened that if they had to withdraw – which was now inevitable – and the partisans attacked them as they retreated, the cities of Bologna, Reggio Emilia, Parma and Piacenza would be destroyed. If the partisans did not attack the Germans, the cities and their inhabitants would be spared. The Germans wanted an answer by 2 March, but the partisans refused to deal with them. In the event the Germans never carried out their threat.

The Repubblichini, too, knew that their last hour was near. Many of them were the scourings of the jails, and they began to be even more vile than before, burning houses, torturing people, and retaliating against the civilian population in every way they could. Early one morning, just before the end, they threw grenades at the front of our house. Fortunately no one was injured.

That unbelievable, unforgettable April finally came. People called it the Primavera della Patria, the Rebirth of the Country. On 18 April the German garrison fled from Fontanellato. In Parma the Germans and Fascists began to leave in the early hours of the morning. On the subject of all these movements the radio maintained an obstinate silence.

German troops passed through Fontanellato by any means

174

they could, using the side roads in an attempt to avoid being bombed and machine-gunned. They tried to reach the River Po, which they hoped to cross so that they could eventually get back to Germany. In the middle of the night and all through the day there were constant knocks on the door from desperate soldiers who wanted bicycles. Some demanded them at gunpoint, but we had hidden ours and my parents explained in German that they had already been taken.

On 23 April the Allies reached the Po north of Bologna, which had been liberated during the night of 21–2 April. At 22.25 on the twenty-fifth, the American Fifth Army entered Parma and the streets were full of partisans. We were free. Parma went mad: there was a tremendous and indescribable exultation. From the windows of every house, white sheets hung out instead of flags.

The Americans came to Fontanellato too, and all the girls gathered bunches of flowers to throw to the liberators. But to everyone's great disappointment they showed hardly any signs of pleasure. They stopped their vehicles, talked very little, and chewed gum. Perhaps they were tired. Perhaps they had liberated too many places like Fontanellato. But we were disappointed.

It was hard to adjust to a normal life; to no longer fearing that the door would suddenly be opened and somebody would come to take us away; to the thought that there might soon be more food; and that we might be able to travel further afield than Parma or even Trieste.

But although I was happy there were two questions I couldn't stop thinking about. The most important was, what had happened to Eric? And the other, who had denounced my father? I couldn't be at peace until I knew the answers to these. I felt sure that if Eric was alive he would write, although friends thought he would never appear again. Perhaps, they said, he was married or engaged and had not

175

told me the truth about himself. As for my father, I was convinced that sooner or later local Fascists would be arrested and made to confess some of their crimes.

During the Repubblichini period there had been a Secretary to the Party in Fontanellato. He was a senior, dedicated member, and it didn't at first appear that he had committed any atrocities, but we later found out that he was responsible for denouncing people who had anti-Fascist sympathies, and that it was because of him that we had been taken to Tabiano. He was arrested and kept in the town hall in Fontanellato. As soon as I heard this, I went there and found his room. Without permission, I opened the door and saw him sitting on a chair, guarded by a partisan. I looked coldly into his eyes and said very slowly: 'You are the bastard who denounced my father and were responsible for all of us being taken to Tabiano. Thanks to you we might be dead.' I took in his frightened expression and could just faintly hear his reply: '*Non è vero*' – 'It isn't true.'

I didn't want to hear any more. I slapped his face and left. It was something I had never done before and never would again, and it gave me great satisfaction.

Slowly life in Fontanellato returned to normal. Soldiers began to leave for home (although many never left), rationing became less strict, the *balere* reopened (a great event for the young) and, most important of all, we could talk freely without the fear of being overheard. The cafés were full once again; men drank and played cards and talked endlessly about the war. The Fontanellatesi, like all Italians, felt happy; happy that they had stood up to the Fascists, and happy that they had helped the escaped prisoners.

That summer the Allies announced that the families who had helped prisoners-of-war would be remunerated for the board and lodging they had given: a form could be collected from the town hall. Although my family hadn't sheltered any

176

prisoners-of-war, we had provided food and clothing, so we too could claim. But the amount of money we received would have been so little that we thought it would be far more useful if instead I could be given a job in one of the innumerable Allied offices that had sprung up everywhere. I would receive a salary and be able to practise my English. I filled in the form with this request instead of a claim for money, although I didn't have much hope that anything would happen.

One day a young, moustached British officer arrived in a jeep and asked people in the village where I lived. I was in the bank, so he came to see me there and introduced himself. 'If I am correct, you have applied for a job with the British. I have come to offer you one with the Allied Screening Commission in Verona. The job will be connected with helping Italians who hid or otherwise helped prisoners-of-war.'

Verona was far away and I had never lived away from home; besides, I was not sure that my parents had ever contemplated the possibility that I might do so. They had been thinking of a job in Parma to which I would commute daily; but this one sounded very interesting, something after my own heart.

'My parents will never allow me to go to Verona,' I answered. 'In Italy young women live with their families; it is unheard-of for them to leave home.'

Captain Taylor, for this was the officer's name, was adamant. 'Why don't we go to see your parents and discuss the matter with them?' We went and we discussed. Taylor made use of all his persuasive charm.

'Your daughter will be in good hands. She will work with the Allied Screening Commission which is part of M.I.9, and she will live with a charming couple, Signor and Signora Banterle. Signor Banterle is an architect and they live in a beautiful villa which overlooks all Verona. Not only will your daughter be able to come home whenever she wishes, but we will also provide transport.'

It was difficult to refuse. The next morning I had to give in my notice at the bank – first to the manager at Fontanellato and then, in person, to my boss in Parma. One week later Captain Taylor came to fetch me in a jeep. I had packed my case in a state of some excitement, taking only my best clothes with me. They were very few. Then I had said goodbye to all my friends. Nora had commented: 'If your house burns down you will never burn inside. You are always out.'

All this time I had had to try hard not to think of what my parents must have been feeling about my going away. I knew that they would be criticized by the Fontanellatesi for allowing me to go away and live in a distant city among thousands of Allied soldiers. Perhaps I was one of the first women in the entire province of Parma to be 'liberated' in that sense.

It was bitterly cold in the open jeep, but Taylor had brought an army greatcoat for me to wear. I felt a bit like a Circassian slave being taken to Constantinople. He asked me whether I would prefer to see Bologna and spend the night there, or to drive directly to Verona. As it had been years since I had been anywhere further away from Fontanellato than Parma, I had no hesitation in saying that I would like to go to Bologna.

It was late in the afternoon when we arrived, and Taylor took me for a drive through the town, which apart from the centre had been badly damaged. We went on to the villa which had been requisitioned for the Bologna branch of the Allied Screening Commission: like all the villas requisitioned by Germans and members of the Allied forces alike, it was far too splendid for the purpose to which they put it.

The following morning we set off for Verona. Almost the entire journey was through the plain, now covered in dense fog. Then, suddenly, we found ourselves in brilliant sunshine at the southern outskirts of the city, at the foot of the pre-Alps, where the River Adige emerges into the plain. It was in these industrial areas on the east side of the city that the damage caused by Allied bombing had been most extensive. Verona had suffered more than thirty major raids. During their retreat, the Germans had added to the destruction by blowing up all ten of the bridges over the river: where these had been, the riverbed was partially blocked by great piles of masonry. We drove up one of the steep hills which look down on the city and are encircled by walls and bastions (built by the great sixteenth-century architect Michele Sanmichele) to the house where I was going to live.

Signor and Signora Banterle were anxious to see what sort of strange guest had been picked for them, and I was equally anxious to find out about them – especially after some of the experiences of my schooldays in Parma. There was no need to fear. The Signore was extrovert and jolly and his wife was a wonderful cook, and very soon I was considered as one of the family. The Signore had designed the house himself along the lines of a Palladian villa in Vicenza, choosing a site that gave a most remarkable view of the city spread out below. Although the house had only one floor it was rather grandiose, and full of pretentious-looking reproduction Renaissance furniture which was distinctly uncomfortable to live with. Nevertheless it was a house of which I was to have very happy memories.

The first days and weeks of my new job were difficult both for me and for my employers, because my English, when it came to the test, was still very elementary. I had done my best to study the language in Fontanellato. I had quite a good vocabulary and had written letters to Eric, but I hadn't had anyone to talk to in English. In spite of my difficulties, all the officers and men showed great kindness and patience;

except for one Australian officer who did not disguise the fact that he would have been only too happy to send me back to where I had come from. Fortunately his rude manners did not cut much ice with his colleagues either. I got on much better with one of the corporals, Corporal House, who was the cook. As I was permanently hungry, he used to make enormous treacle puddings – it was the first time in my life I had heard of such a dish – and always made sure I got a big helping. He also gave me whole tins of peaches in syrup; I ate so many that eventually I broke out in a painful rash. In spite of all this food I remained as thin as a rake, and was as hungry as ever.

The British soldiers, both the officers and the rank and file, seemed to be very popular with the inhabitants of Verona. They formed clubs and held tea dances to which local girls were invited. I went often, partly because I enjoyed dancing and partly because we were offered the most delicious cakes, of a sort that was almost impossible to obtain except on the black market. Tea dances with cakes; it all sounds rather dull in 1991, but to us then the cakes were manna from heaven and the dances were the greatest of fun. I was aware that in some circles there was a market for less innocuous pleasures, for there was a great deal of poverty that winter, and the occupying armies, with their apparently endless supplies of food and tobacco and warm clothes, could buy more or less whatever they wanted.

By this time I was beginning to think that Eric was either dead or had chosen to forget me, and I felt very depressed. I had always considered him, and still did in the absence of any other evidence, to be a sincere person, one who would do anything to fulfil his promises. It was true that he had never said he would marry me, but he had said that when the war was over he would write to me and try to come back.

180

Now I began to wonder if my friends had not been right when they said I would never see him again.

By the time I had almost given up hope, a telegram arrived. It read: 'I am safe, I love you and will be with you for Christmas.' I read it and reread it, again and again. I couldn't believe it was true.

A couple of weeks later, just as most of the officers and men of the Allied Screening Commission in Verona were preparing to go off for the weekend to the country, an enormous, chauffeur-driven Fiat motor car with a flag on the front of it rolled up in the drive. It was the largest Fiat anyone had ever seen (and was, in fact, one of a small number commissioned by the Fascists for the use of Mussolini and other top members of the hierarchy). Panic broke out. Obviously the car must contain some high-ranking officer, probably a general, who would not be at all pleased to find an important branch of M.I.9 in the process of closing itself down for the weekend early on a Saturday morning.

What emerged from this astonishing machine was Eric, wearing a wonderful sheepskin coat and boots. He had known where I was because he had received all my letters, although I hadn't received any of his. (They all arrived together at Fontanellato the following week, after getting stuck in some military censor's office.)

By pure chance, while walking up a street in London, Eric had met a friend who had invited him into White's Club for a drink. There, at the bar, he had been introduced to one of the heads of M.I.9 who, when he heard that Eric wanted to get back to Italy and could speak more Italian than most people who had been on the run, immediately offered to make him a member of the Allied Screening Commission. The details had been agreed at the bar.

Two days later Eric had flown to Naples, where he borrowed a jeep from a friend of his, an ex-prisoner from Fon-

tanellato who was now ADC to a general at Caserta, and
drove to Rome, where he reported to his branch of the Commission. From there he begged a lift in a bomber belonging
to the Desert Air Force, and the crew flew him to Udine –
he had been very glad of his sheepskin coat and boots. The
most difficult part of the journey had been the hitch-hike from
Udine to Treviso, but at Treviso he had been lucky enough
to meet the local head of the Allied Military Government,
who occupied another luxurious villa. It was he who had
provided Eric with Mussolini's motor car and a chauffeur.

Looking at him, I couldn't detect much change. Perhaps
after a long and unpleasant time in various German prison
camps in Bavaria, Czechoslovakia and Brunswick, where the
prisoners had been subjected to very severe bombing raids in
which a number of them were killed, he had lost some of his
characteristically boyish expression, but his sense of humour
hadn't suffered. Nor had his optimism, which was a relief to
me as, being a Slav, I am by nature distinctly pessimistic.
When I was talking to Eric anything seemed possible. Even
so, words did not come easily to either of us; for the first time
we both realized how very little we knew about each other.

It was at this point, while we were stumbling about, not
really knowing what to say with so many other people present,
that Eric suggested we should borrow a driver and jeep from
the ASC – this boy was the biggest borrower of jeeps I had
ever met – and set off for Fontanellato, where we could all
be reunited: my parents, the Merlis, the Superiora and the
suore at the hospital, and as many of the other people who
had helped him as possible, including Dr Sambataro, of whom
there had been no news since he joined the partisans. On
Sunday night the driver would take me back to Verona and
Eric would somehow get to Rome, where he was going to be
working.

It turned out to be a difficult journey. Because the Germans had blown the bridges over the Po, there were only temporary bridges with long queues of vehicles waiting to cross them. That evening, as we walked through the village that Eric had never seen on our way to the orphanage, I felt proud and happy that he had come back. Later we went into the darkness of the Santuario; there was no one there but the Madonna, who seemed to look down benignly on us as for centuries she had looked on friend and enemy alike.

The following morning we went to see the beautiful, fifteenth-century stables of the Sanvitale castle, and there, under the arcades, Eric asked me to marry him. I knew nothing at all about England, apart from what I had gathered from reading a number of the works of P.G. Wodehouse translated into Italian; and not even someone as ignorant as I was could possibly have believed that Wodehouse's England was the England I would find. Nevertheless, although I knew that there would be no Castello di Blandings awaiting me – Eric had always gone to great lengths to tell me that his family was not at all grand or well-off – I said yes.

Then he went back to Rome and I returned to Verona.

From now on we had the greatest difficulty in talking to one another, let alone meeting. The only way Eric could telephone me was by using a military line via Bologna and Vienna, which took hours on end, and even when he'd got through, our voices were often unintelligible. It seemed impossible then that Italy could ever recover from the damage it had suffered. There were no bridges left standing between Verona and Rome and, according to Eric, who from now on was to travel this way once a week, every village south of Florence on the main road to Viterbo and Rome had been either destroyed or severely damaged. The churches had suffered particularly badly. The tally of religious paintings and statues lost was immense. Everything was broken; it is difficult now to imagine the devastation. I shall always remember the cold of that winter of 1945, the first winter after the war. The whole of the *pianura* was covered in freezing fog that struck into the marrow of my bones in a way that no cold has ever done since. It was exactly as I had always imagined the Dark Ages to be, and in its terrible way it was apt.

Each Saturday morning Eric would fly to Udine from Rome in one of the Desert Air Force bombers, in which he nearly froze to death, then hitch a lift from there to Verona – the huge Fiat was not part of the service. We would spend the afternoon walking through the streets of Verona in the twilight which, with the prevailing fog, lasted most of the afternoon. The architect and his wife would put Eric up for the night and give us both a delicious dinner, the Signora exercising just the degree of chaperonage that was considered desirable at that time. On Sunday morning Eric and I would make a trip into the pre-Alpine hills behind Verona and eat a delicious simple meal, which was all that was available at that time, in a *trattoria*. Then, in the late afternoon, Eric would be picked up by the US postal jeep, which carried important military mail from Milan to Rome by way of Verona, Bologna and Florence, and arrive in Rome at first light the following morning. It was not a comfortable journey. There were two GIs in charge – the driver and a sentry guard – and Eric had to sit on top of a pile of waterproof mailbags. The jeep was fitted with a snorkel so that it could cross the streams and rivers encountered on the way.

A far greater problem than the journey from Rome to Verona and back was our plan to get married – which I was gradually getting used to. A marriage between foreign nationals from different countries and of different religions would have been difficult enough in settled times, but it was rendered much more complicated now by the fact that whatever my family's record might have been with regard to the Fascist Party, my mother, my father and I were enemy

184

aliens who had just lost a war. The authorities – in this case the military authorities – were extremely reluctant to allow members of the armed forces to contract such marriages, and made it as difficult as possible for anyone wishing to do so. At the time it seemed senselessly cruel, but it often proved justifiable in the end: some girls who married Englishmen or Americans found themselves very unhappy in their new life, and eventually returned to Italy.

Whatever the rights and wrongs of the matter, the authorities required from me a birth certificate from Štanjel, a certificate of Italian citizenship, a certificate from a bishop declaring that I was *stato libero* so far as marriage was concerned, and goodness knows what else. They even demanded that I take a Wassermann test in order to be sure that I wasn't suffering from syphilis. To clear this last hurdle I was forced to queue up outside a shed with a number of soldiers. It very nearly made me give up the entire project.

Eric's parents, who, according to him, could scarcely be regarded as enthusiastic churchgoers, now developed a strong feeling that any children that might result from our marriage ought to be brought up as members of the Church of England. I didn't like the idea of this at all.

Caught in what promised to be a whirlpool of conflicting dogmatic beliefs, Eric, who didn't care either way so long as I was happy, went off to see Mgr O'Flaherty, a well-known priest who had given help and shelter to large numbers of escaping prisoners-of-war and was now an important figure in the Holy Office. O'Flaherty told Eric that he didn't mind which way we brought up our children either, provided they were baptized as Catholics. With this inscrutable answer everyone was apparently content.

A far worse impediment was the Colonel in command of the Allied Screening Commission. He had been Senior British Officer in command of the prisoners in the orphanage and he had received considerable help from the people of Fontanellato; eventually he had been helped to reach Switzerland. Now, suddenly, a few months before the date we had settled on for our marriage, he began to worry about the idea of one of his officers (who made no claims to any sort of upper-class lineage) marrying the daughter of a village schoolmaster. He did everything he could to make it impossible for the marriage to take place. Fortunately the two of us were too much for him.

The time had now come for Eric to go up into the Apennines on behalf of the Commission to pay and honour all those Italians, for the most part peasants, who had helped and in many cases saved the lives of escaping prisoners-of-war. I was sent with him to keep the accounts. We set off in an open 15-cwt. truck with an Italian driver who had also been a soldier, two Schmeisser machine pistols and a lot of ammunition; the mountains at that time were infested with bandits, some of whom were Allied and Axis deserters. We also had with us an immensely heavy steel strongbox which contained enormous quantities of devalued lire. The whole operation of recognizing the bravery of the Italians who had helped prisoners-of-war turned out to be an utter disaster, not only in Eric's area but throughout the country. The amount of money paid out depended on how many hours, days or weeks a prisoner had been helped or sheltered for. It was impossible by this method to take into account the question of whether one situation was more dangerous than another. Far worse than this was a decree issued by the British Treasury to the effect that all money paid out was to be at the old pre-invasion rate of 72 lire to the pound; the rate in 1945 was actually 1760 lire to the pound. This meant that some of those who qualified for money received literally nothing at all. Even the certificate of merit, thanking the recipient for his or her efforts, proved to be a Roneoed sheet of office paper bearing a typewritten message and a completely unconvincing reproduction of Field Marshal Alexander's signature as Commander-in-Chief. In many cases Eric found himself unable to hand over such miserable rewards to *contadini* who had risked their lives helping prisoners. The three of us often went off to ordnance depots where Eric bent all his efforts to persuading whoever was in charge to donate a load of blankets (which made excellent winter coats and suits) or, if he was trying to help a doctor, a set of motor tyres, which were worth their weight in gold.

We were eventually married in the spring of 1946, in the Church of Santa Croce in Florence. The ceremony took place in the Bardi Chapel, which is decorated with Giotto's great frescoes depicting the life of St Francis of Assisi. A few days later I would be leaving for England. Eric would have to travel in a military train. As we walked out arm in arm, under the high timber roof, I wondered what the future held in store.